Elsie Cressman
A Trailblazing Life

Elsie Cressman
A Trailblazing Life

by
Nancy Silcox

PANDORA
PRESS

Library and Archives Canada Cataloguing in Publication

Silcox, Nancy, 1949-
Elsie Cressman : a trailblazing life / by Nancy Silcox.

ISBN 978-1-926599-27-4

1. Cressman, Elsie. 2. Cressman, Elsie--Trials, litigation, etc. 3. Midwives--Canada--Biography. 4. Malpractice--Canada--Case studies. I. Title.

RG950.S54 2013 618.20092 C2013-901078-5

Book and cover design by Christian Snyder

ELSIE CRESSMAN.
ISBN 978-1-926599-27-4

Published by Pandora Press

www.pandorapress.com

20 19 18 17 16 15 14 13 2 3 4 5 6 7 8 9 10

Table of Contents

PREFACE

In January 2002 the trial of midwife Elsie Cressman commenced in a Kitchener courthouse. More than four years had passed since Elsie had learned that she was being sued for malpractice for a delivery some years before. The boy, Paul Carere, had cerebral palsy and suffered from a number of other physical and intellectual disabilities.

Paul's parents, Christine and Fred Carere, charged that midwife Elsie Cressman had shown negligence and failure to give informed consent to Christine during Elsie's attempt to turn the fetus which was laying in a breech position. These actions had contributed to Paul's premature birth and present condition. The Careres were asking for more than five million dollars in damages for this claim.

When news of the suit was made public, Elsie's peers, friends and former clients were shocked and dismayed. They flooded her with telephone calls, cards and letters of support. Many wrote letters of outrage to the local newspaper. A former colleague, midwife Francesca Gee wrote:

> I had the privilege of working with Elsie in the 1980's and knew her to be one of the most knowledgeable, compassionate and tireless midwives in the profession. Lessons learned from her mentoring continue to inform my practice some fourteen years later.

Another letter to the editor came from university professor, and former midwifery client, Dr. Carol Ann Weaver:

> Elsie Cressman is arguably the most celebrated midwife in Canada. She holds the prestigious Order of Ontario award, plus an earned RN certification, and has more experience than possibly any Canadian midwife alive today. She is reaching her later years now and I feel that this is a time to treat her with the utmost respect, not to

cloud her reputation with harsh press releases.

Supporters notwithstanding, the charge would be heard in a Kitchener courtroom – date to be determined. Few imagined at the time that the just-retired midwife legend would need to wait four years to try to clear her name – and reputation.

Part One

Family Roots

Chapter One
Swiss Mennonite Family Roots

In the early 1700's, one Nicholaus Cressman,[1] a Swiss farmer and Mennonite made a momentous decision. Seeking religious freedom and land – more than he and others of his kin could dream of owning in their tiny mountainous homeland – Nicholaus gathered up his life savings and bid goodbye to friends and family. He was going to America, the land of opportunity and plenty.

Arriving in the bustling harbour of New York City, perhaps Boston or Baltimore, the traveler continued west to the wide open spaces and rolling hills of Pennsylvania. He settled in Limerick County, where other Amish or Mennonite brethren had settled before him. Through hard work and opportunity Nicholaus prospered.

But the early 1800's, land had again become an issue. The northeastern states were now heavily populated and farm land was at a premium. Farmers were moving north to British North America where land was to be had for a song. In 1806, Abraham Cressman, four generations removed from the pioneering Nicholaus packed his worldly possessions into an oxen-drawn cart and joined the exodus.

A number of his brethren had settled around the village of Strasburg, in southern Ontario, and it was here that Abraham Cressman also ended his long journey. In Strasburg he married and fathered twelve children. His eldest son Daniel was the first of the family line to be Canadian-born. After Daniel's marriage, he moved with his wife to a farm on Concession 3 of Wilmot Township, southeast of the village of New Hamburg in Waterloo County.

To this point, the Cressmans had not yet taken leadership roles in their church community, one of the "conservative Mennonite" denominations. Daniel's eldest son, Menno would alter that. In 1869, Menno Cressman was ordained as Deacon of the Community

[1] Koch, Alice. *Descendants of Menno Cressman*, (n.p., 1990).

Mennonite body. In 1870 he was called to the Ministry.

The Cressmans prospered financially too. In 1875, Menno purchased a 121-acre farm in the southeast corner of the township and ran this operation along with the home farm. His eldest son, Ezra (Elsie's grandfather), born in 1860 was his father's designate to take over this farm.

In 1880, Ezra married the former Louisa Shantz, and as was the custom, the couple set up housekeeping with Ezra's parents. Once construction of a new home on the second farm was complete, they would set up housekeeping there. Three sons were born to Ezra and Louisa Cressman: Leander, in 1887; Curtis (Elsie's father) in 1894 and Howard in 1897.

Unlike royalty, Mennonite tradition usually held that the youngest son of a farming family inherited the "family jewels" – the ancestral farm. So it was expected that Howard would eventually take over the home farm. Leander and Curtis would make their ways independently.

Chapter Two
Curtis to the Church

From an early age, Curtis Cressman had taken great interest in his church, Biehn Mennonite, on the outskirts of New Hamburg. The Biehn congregation viewed themselves as "conservative" Mennonites. Not as rigid in their beliefs and expressions of faith as the Old Order sects who rejected all types of modernity, women of the Biehn congregation still wore head coverings and print dresses with bosom-hiding "capes."

He had been inspired by the preaching of notable Mennonite evangelists who regularly came to address the Biehn congregation. As he matured, Curtis took on church leadership roles, speaking at services and other church meetings. Quiet and serious, intelligent and articulate, Curtis would still speak his mind when needed. And others would listen. "It was natural that the elders of the church would mark him for important things," says Elsie.

In 1916, at the young age of twenty-two, Curtis was ordained and selected to become a Minister for the Biehn congregation. By mutual consent between the young man, his family and the church, it was agreed that he should receive further education and leadership teachings, before taking up his post. With few if any Mennonite institutions providing such training in Canada, Curtis would attend Hesston Mennonite College in Kansas. He left for the United States in late 1916. If all went well he would return in two years to take up his pastorship.

When Curtis left for the United States of America, the world had been at war for two years. Young Canadians and Americans were fighting on the battlefields of France, Holland, Belgium and Germany. Like most of the Mennonite and Amish faith, Curtis declared himself to be a conscientious objector (CO) and requested exemption from front line battle.[1] While some "alternative placements" had been designated for CO's on both sides of the border, exemption was not standard. Many of these objectors were sent, against their will to the front lines. By 1915, in the United States alone, over 2000 Mennonites had been called up to fight.

In 1917, the American Mennonite Church took matters into its own hands and drafted the Selective Service Act.[2] It provided that a CO on the basis of religion would serve in non-combative military roles, such as medics or ambulance attendants. In actuality, the provision proved morally objectionable for most young Mennonite and Amish soldiers, as they were forbidden by their military units to provide medical assistance to any injured enemy soldier they encountered.

Not until March 1918, eight months before the cessation of battle, did the United States Congress enact an Alternative Service provision for religious CO's. For the remainder of the war, they would now serve in such positions as farm hands or labourers. Representatives of a civilian Board of Inquiry would visit various military camps where Mennonites were serving, to hear their individual cases.

Records at the conclusion of the World War I show that almost 4,000 American Mennonites had declared themselves CO's by Armistice in November, 1918. Of those, 1,300 chose non-combative military roles; 1,200 took farm furloughs and 100 went to Europe to do reconstructive work. Yet 450 Mennonite and Amish CO's were court-martialed and sent to Canadian and American prisons, with 950 detained in military camps.[3]

Reports continued to surface, during and after the war, that Mennonites detained in prison and military camps had been subjected to ridicule and abuse for their religious beliefs. Cressman family lore provides a personal story for this ugly chapter of history. Elsie recalls:

---

[1] Yoder, Anne. "World War I Conscientious Objectors." May 2002. www.swarthmore.edu.

[2] Iowa Peacemakers. "The Mennonite and Quaker Example," adapted from an article by Nancy J. T. Guthrie. *The Goldfinch* 13, no. 1 (September, 1991), Iowa City: State Historical Society of Iowa. www.iptv.org/Iowa Pathways/

[3] Penner, Glenn, "Canadian Low-German Mennonites Drafted or Recruited in World War 1," September 2009. www.mennonitegeneology.com.

"my mother's uncle was sent to a military training camp, even though he had declared himself a CO. When he refused to march and hold a gun, he was tortured and tarred and feathered."

Curtis Cressman, of military age when he entered the United States in 1916 was exempt from military service under two provisions: he was a Canadian living in the United States, and he was a student studying for the ministry. He did not serve in any capacity.

Chapter Three
Amanda and the American Bylers

Times had always been tough for Amish-born and raised Jacob and Lydia Byler, and their family of nine children.[1] For this was bone-dry Oklahoma, in the poverty years of the early 1900's. Jacob called himself a farmer. He'd once owned some land, growing a few acres of cotton – when it chose to grow – in the parched soil. For a time, the Bylers lived in an underground dug-out house. With only the roof showing above ground, the accommodation was cool under the summer's parched sun and dusty winds, and cozy when the bitter winds of December came.

But by the time war had broken out in Europe, the property was gone. The Bylers were on the move again, hop-scotching across Oklahoma, Missouri, Arkansas and Kansas, looking for work. Jacob owned a threshing machine and this put him a step above the usual migrant farmer. While jobs were few and paid pennies, Jacob and his trusty thresher never went long without finding some work.

Being Amish helped too. The area was home to various sects of both Mennonite and Amish. And while the two differed in language, dress and customs, they spoke as one when it came to work ethic and comradeship. Many hands made light work, especially during planting and harvest times. Great teams of Amish and Mennonite farmers would travel from neighbourhood to neighbourhood sharing the load. And when Jacob Byler and his threshing machine were in the area, this made the work go even more quickly.

From his earnings Jacob bought a trailer. Now Lydia and the kids could come along too. The vehicle came with a fully-equipped kitchen and Lydia figured she could use this, and her skills as an accomplished cook to earn a bit of money. Working men got hungry fast and why couldn't she provide home-cooking from the kitchen of her mobile home? The scheme met with great success and by the time the couple's

[1] Byler History; Interview with Lillian Richardson Bean, January 2008.

two eldest daughters, Mary and Amanda were in their double-digit years, they were helping their mother too.

School was a now and again thing for the kids of most itinerants like the Bylers. Some learned to read and write, but work always preceded book learning. It was custom too for Mennonite and Amish children to leave school at age 14, sometimes before. Judged now as adults, they joined the working world as farm hands, cooks or other manual laborers.

Cressman-Byler history sees Amanda Byler toiling full-time in her mother's kitchen at the age of 12 or 13. Still this young Amish lass had a good brain and a passion for learning. For her, serving up flapjacks and pork sausage to hungry farmers was just a financial means to an end. Amanda had her eye on becoming a missionary and was saving her earnings to attend Hesston Missionary College in Kansas.

Circa 1916 or 1917, Amanda's dream became reality when she enrolled and began classes there. She soon met a young Canadian named Curtis Cressman. The two became a couple and married after both had graduated in 1919. Curtis was 25 years of age; Amanda was 26. Soon after, they boarded a train for New Hamburg and the Cressman family house.

Elsie recalls that her mother's adjustment to married life was a difficult one. Independent from her own parents since she left for Hesston, she now lived under the roof of Louisa Cressman. And Louisa Cressman was a force to be reckoned with. In Elsie's words:

> Grandmother Louisa was fussy and liked things just so. She was also used to doing things her way. So for someone like my mother, who had her own mind about things, and had been on her own for some time, this must have been very hard. She now had to do things the way her mother-in-law wanted. And no ifs-ands-and buts about it!

The situation was made more onerous for Amanda, given the

limited space that she and Curtis had to call their own. Louisa's rule extended to all but one unheated bedroom where the young couple slept and kept their own belongings.

Nor was Amanda's adjustment solely to the home. A leader in her own circle at Hesston College, Amanda Cressman was a "foreigner," both in religion and nationality, in rural Waterloo County. Elsie distinguishes between the Amish and their "cousins" the Mennonites.

> The Amish had their ways. Their dialect was their own and they dressed differently to us. For example the Amish women always wore aprons, and their dresses were of a solid colour. We Mennonites favoured prints and flowers. The women parted their hair in the Amish way too. As for the men, Mennonites were clean-shaven and Amish wore beards.

And if that was not strange enough, Amanda Byler Cressman was American! Elsie says: "rural folk around where we lived had little use for Americans; in fact I can say that Americans were despised."

No sooner had Curtis returned home, than he dove into preparations for taking the helm of Biehn Mennonite Church. In acceding to this key role in the community, Curtis' wife would play an important part, and was expected to set an example. Given the circumstances in which she found herself, Amanda must have felt considerable unease with these expectations.

Curtis' road was less stony. He quickly gained the confidence of his congregation, and soon came to be well-regarded beyond his own congregation. Within months he had been invited to participate in various committees within the broader Mennonite fellowship; within a decade, Curtis Cressman headed the powerful Mennonite Conference of Ontario. Elsie calls her father "a man who could be counted on to make good decisions."

Ironically, though Curtis was an influential and powerful man, he drew neither salary nor living allowance from his position. For income, he needed to take up the only other livelihood he knew – farming. The mix was not a fruitful one. With chuch duties taking prominence in mind and time, Curtis spent minimal time in his barn or on his land. "So we were poor," Elsie says, "because Dad never had time to make any money."

The money issue became more pressing when in 1920, Amanda gave birth to her first child, a son. The baby died soon after birth. In reflecting back on this tragedy, Elsie is vocal about the circumstances. "He was born in that bitter cold room where my parents slept and he was pulled out by forceps." She leaves unsaid the loneliness and isolation that her mother must have felt during this time.

One year later Amanda gave birth again, this time to a healthy daughter, Ruth. On April 13, 1923 the couple's second daughter, Elsie, entered the world. In 1924, a son Howard was born. Around this time Curtis, Amanda and their children left the family farm. Curtis had purchased a 100-acre farm in adjacent Oxford County, several miles to the south of the family homestead. With this relocation, and Ezra and Louisa's retirement into New Hamburg, Curtis' younger brother, Howard finally fulfilled his destiny and took possession of the Cressman ancestral farm.

For the three sons of Ezra and Louisa Cressman, now married with families, and settled on properties of their own, with hard work and a bit of luck, prosperity might have shone its light on their faces. This was not to be. Howard contracted pneumonia in 1927. The illness then was a virtual death sentence, and most pneumonia patients died. Howard was no exception and passed away at the tender age of thirty. His widow Ida was forced to auction off the farm equipment and livestock. She then sold the farm for far less than it was worth. Ida then returned to her parents' home.

The farm's purchasers soon went belly-up too and were unable to meet mortgage payments. In these dire circumstances, Ezra Cressman, the mortgage holder stepped up. Elsie comments on her grandfather's financial affairs:

> Grandfather Ezra was kind and had, over the years, given his money to people who asked for it. So now he had little left for himself. He and Grandma Louisa had no choice now but to sell their retirement home in New Hamburg and move back to the family farm again.

Leander Cressman's misfortune next came calling.[1] In the summer of 1929, he had purchased one-hundred head of young cattle, thinking to fatten them over the winter and sell them in the spring at a healthy profit. With the September 1929 Stock Market crash, prices of grain soared and beef prices plummeted. Leander was left with animals he couldn't feed or market. He resorted to selling the stock at a great loss. But more disaster was on the horizon. In desperate financial straits, he was unable to make the mortgage payments on his own farm. With the loss of his property looming, Leander asked his father to take over the mortgage. Ezra refused.

More than eighty years after this tragic situation, one which opened long-standing and profound family wounds, Ezra Cressman's hard decision continues to stir debate with surviving members of the family and allegiances remain divided. Leander's family sees Ezra's actions as stemming from his disapproval of Leander marrying outside the Mennonite religion.* Curtis' descendants see his motives differently: Elsie says: "these were bad times and Leander was not a successful farmer to begin with. Grandpa Ezra did what he had to do."

Leander, his wife Jessie, and their five young children were now homeless. They found accommodation with a neighbouring farmer and Leander set himself the task of earning a living as a butcher. Still tragedy had not yet paid its final call on the door of Leander Cressman. In 1932, his vehicle was hit by a trolley car as it crossed over train tracks. He was killed instantly. Leander Cressman was forty-five years old.

Nor did tough times overlook Curtis and Amanda Cressman.

---

[1] Interview with the late Marie Cressman Shantz, February-April 2008.

During the Depression, they too lost their farm and were forced to return to the family homestead.

As the Depression years gave way to the darkening years leading up to World War II, the Cressman family fortunes recovered. Ezra became one of the first farmers in the New Hamburg area to purchase an automobile. Not that the old gentleman would drive the new-fangled machine, but it was fun to own one nevertheless! He enjoyed taking a drive with one of his sons behind the wheel.

A favourite family story sees Ezra asking his son Curtis to take him for a spin to the barber shop. And on the way back maybe they'd have time to stop at a neighbour's farm. Ezra, a great horse fancier wanted to see a new mare the man had just acquired.

Ezra never got a chance to see that new mare. In the barber's chair, he suffered a massive heart attack and died. "We all knew how disappointed Grandpa must have been not to get a chance to see that fine horse," Elsie chuckles.

Chapter Four
Fun on the Farm

The person who would hold the most influence over young Elsie Cressman wasn't blood family at all, but a young orphaned girl, with a sad past named Lillian Richardson.

Lillian, now 99 and a resident at Nithview Retirement Home in New Hamburg recalls the little she knows about her natural parents.

> My parents, George and Carol Richardson, along with my four brothers and sisters had immigrated to Canada from England in 1910. Mom had respiratory problems and they hoped that the Canadian climate and medical care would help her. I believe that they settled in the Niagara Region around Hamilton and my Dad found work as a stone mason. I was born in Hamilton in 1912.

Within a year of Lillian's birth, Carol died. George, left with a family of five, had no other option than to look for homes for his children. "He hoped that he'd be able to bring us back as a family," Lillian says, with a catch in her voice. George Richardson's dream was never fulfilled. He died two years after arriving in Canada of complications from malaria, contracted years before, while fighting in the South African Boer War.

Lillian's sister was sent to a foster home in Galt; her brothers to a foster family, the Nahrgangs in New Hamburg. Lillian, only a few months old at the time was fostered by the Thorgoods, an older couple whose children were grown. She remained with them until she was eight years of age. By this time, she confesses, "I'd grown cute and bad, and was too much of a handful." She was sent to an orphanage for "training."

For the next year, Lillian was shuttled between several foster homes and the orphanage. "And I grew into even more of a handful; I said whatever I thought, and was very outspoken." Eventually, she was sent to the Nahrgangs. Orphanage officials reasoned that being with her brothers would settle her.

The Nahrgangs, with Richardson children in tow, attended Biehn Mennonite Church outside New Hamburg. It was here that young Lilliam first set eyes on Amanda Cressman.

> I took a shine to her and within several times of seeing her, I decided that I wanted to live in her house. So bold one that I was, I walked right up to her at church and asked if she would take me home to live with her. She was startled but didn't brush me off.

And so the tiny girl with the big past entered Curtis and Amanda Cressman's life – and stayed. She was enrolled at the nearby Green's School and completed her grade eight education there. Then she filled the role of nanny to her foster brothers and sisters – Ruth, Elsie and Howard. "I was happy and had a natural love of little babies," Lillian recalls with fondness. While her wild ways continued to surface from time to time, with a newfound stability in her life, Lillian matured into responsibility.

"As a child," Elsie reflects, "I was happiest when I was outside or in the barn caring for the animals." And farm animals there were a-plenty to fill her nurturing needs. Joining the requisite cattle and workhorses in the Cressman barnyard were chickens, geese, ducks, cats and dogs. The dependable workhorses, Jean and Nellie provide her clearest childhood memories. "Before I'd even started school, I was riding them – huge animals that they were. I'd hold on to their manes and ride them around the property." Endless litters of barn kittens offered warm and breathing (if uncooperative) victims for playing "babies."

When Elsie was eight or nine, Curtis came home from a farm auction with two pairs of baby goslings. He asked Elsie if she'd like to raise them.

> I was keen and set out to do the best job I could. I set the goslings under the hens to keep warm until they grew. When the females began laying eggs, I put baskets over them at night to make sure they stayed on the nest. I'd decided I would raise their goslings too. Before I knew it, I had twenty females hatching eggs. By the end of the first year, I had seventy-two geese running around the barnyard.

Elsie made some pocket money selling the birds to friends and family for special Christmas and Easter meals. With that many animals under her charge, there were sure to be injuries. Farm livestock became Elsie's first nursing patients. A young gosling, whose foot had been stepped on by a horse became her first patient.

> The gosling's foot was pretty mangled, but I thought I could fix it. I dipped a bandage in some medicinal solution, made a splint and wrapped the foot up. It never healed properly, but the bird could get around and not be attacked by the others.

Doll play also brought out Elsie's mothering traits. Her favourite was a large, soft cloth doll. She and her first cousin Marie Cressman were "the best doll players" and spent hours mothering their babies. "We were especially good at making them cry," Elsie laughs.

On one particular occasion, she had been visiting at Marie's house, a good five or six country miles away. When the time came for Elsie to be taken home in the buggy, Marie's brothers, Alan and Bob were enlisted for the job. Marie would come along. The boys got more than they bargained for on this trip.

> Marie and I insisted that our "babies" ride up front with the boys. In fact we'd even decided that they sit on the boys' knees so they could see better. Not surprisingly the boys refused. Of course they would have been horrified if someone saw them with dolls on their laps. But Marie and I kicked up such a fuss that Aunt Jessie gave in and

> told the boys to ride with the dolls. We weren't popular with either of them for a long time after that.

Cousin to cousin doll-playing was one of the few "girly" activities Elsie took part in. In most ways she was an inveterate tomboy. "I liked being with Howard and my boy cousins, and had more in common with them than Ruth, who was pretty quiet and studious."

Elsie preferred being outdoors and active. Outdoor play was simple, and make-do on a farm in Waterloo County in the late 1920's. Play was walking on stilts, rolling an iron wheel over and over down the hill into the river, watching the water in the creek seep over rubber boots, and digging to China through the sawdust in the ice house.

Time with foster sister Lillian was exciting too. Young Lillian walked on the wild side of life, and Elsie was fascinated by the older girl's antics.

> Lillian was good but she was naughty too. Once she stuck her fingers in all the jars of jam that Mother had made. They were ruined. And by the time I was five or six, she'd become boy crazy too. Mother tried but just couldn't handle her.

It was Curtis who went to bat with his wife for Lillian. He had a soft spot in his heart for the orphan with the sad past. Amanda came to care for her foster daughter too. "She became the best helper Mom could ever have had," Elsie says. As for the three Cressman children? "Lillian spoiled us to death, and we grew to love her dearly."

Dolls and fun with the boys happily filled Elsie's time, but she still felt something was missing in her life. "Oh. I wanted a baby brother or baby sister so badly after Howard grew into a toddler," she says. So she was delighted, around 1928 or 1929, to learn that her mother was expecting again.

Amanda Cressman had had two miscarriages after Howard's birth, but this time things seemed to be progressing favourably. Still, her health was delicate. She'd shown symptoms of diabetes for some time, but treatment was ineffective in those early days. Insulin had been discovered but remained unproven so physicians did not insist on it for their diabetic patients. Many, including Amanda Cressman preferred to self-doctor.

Despite these concerns, as Amanda's pregnancy continued, this time it looked like a new Cressman would join the family. But then the baby was stillborn. Amanda's grief was only matched by her middle daughter's, who was devastated.

> I began to bug Mother to adopt a baby. I kept at it, and at it, and begged and begged. But it was no use. By this time Mother was not well. Her diabetes was getting worse and there was absolutely no chance she was strong enough to look after any baby – one she had borne or one we'd adopted.

Chapter Five
School Days

The Curtis Cressman family was more learned than most among the farming folk of the area. Curtis would in time become a Bishop of the Mennonite Church. Despite her early interrupted education, Amanda had graduated from Hesston College, a rarity among women at the time. As Pastor's wife, she was also expected to set an example for her husband's parishioners. Amanda spoke at various women's assemblies, and gave readings at Mennonite young people's groups. "But she never got over the stigma of being an American," Elsie states, "and this held her back in the community."

It would follow logically, given their parents leanings' that the Cressman children would be scholarly, and Ruth fit the mold. With a laugh, Elsie admits that she was anything but a good student at S.S. #4, Green's Corner Public School, the one-room school where all three Cressmans attended:

> I was terrible and mischievous. More than once, the girl who sat in front of me found her braids in my inkwell. So I stood in the corner a lot, certainly more than most girls. I think I was bored, not because I was so smart or that the work was too easy, but I found it hard to sit in a desk for hours at a time. I needed to be moving, preferably outside.

Despite her delinquencies, Elsie Cressman had real leadership qualities. She was an organizer and loved to get groups of classmates together to perform concerts, plays and recitations. Time and maturity eventually took care of the mischievousness and Elsie settled into the routine of school. Never a scholar, always a participator, Elsie's elementary school career ended with grade eight graduation in 1937.

As was customary in Mennonite households, she looked forward to a year at home before charting her educational future. Ruth had remained at home after her grade eight year, and now Elsie joined her. Ruth was not certain if she'd continue on with her studies, and at the start of her own "sabbatical," Elsie was thinking on the same lines. "I thought it would be great, not having to sit at a desk, being able to be active and busy outside at home."

The girls were kept busy assisting her mother with housework, and helped to care for grandparents, Ezra and Louisa, who after their financial losses, lived in one end of the home. Elsie, the outdoors girl, also pitched in with barn and field chores. But eventually the scent faded from the fourteen-year-old's rose.

> I soon got very bored with being home, with the same things to do, day in and day out. I realized that if I didn't go back to school this is what I'd look forward to – a life of boring housework. And that was not what I wanted!

As Elsie's year at home ground on, she began to talk of returning to high school. Plattsville Continuation School, a good five miles distant, was the closest. Curtis was not convinced of his middle daughter's commitment to school, having seen her past academic nonchalance. But in her mother, Elsie found an ally. Amanda had been forced to leave school before she wished, and she now pushed for Elsie's education. Curtis acquiesced when Elsie informed him that a neighbour girl would be attending Plattsville too. The two girls could share the buggy driving. "She could drive one day and I could the other," Elsie says. The arrangement worked well, with the girls taking turns going out at lunch to give their "taxi" a bag of oats. The horse boarded during the school day at a farm near the school.

Elsie had matured and liked high school. She has fond memories of both the academics and extra-curricular activities.

> It was a very small school and the grade nine and ten students, all ten of us, were together in one class. I liked Science best, English least. At lunch we played sports, ball in the summer and volleyball in the winter. I always

> participated, but wasn't good at sports. My sense of direction was never that strong.

Her sister's enthusiasm persuaded Ruth that she should reconsider her future. She made plans to enroll at Plattsville the next academic year.

Elsie might have completed her education at Plattsville had her parents not been returning from a trip to the US near the end of her grade nine year. They had stopped in the little town of Fort Erie, very close to the US-Canada border, and by chance, had occasion to visit the Ontario Bible School there. Both were impressed by its Christian tone and reputation, and praised it to their children when they arrived home.

Elsie was particularly taken by what she heard. "My friend Beulah Snyder went there and she loved it. She said that the kids who went there were so nice. I told my Mother and Father that I would love to go." Elsie's parents said they would look into having her attend. She was over the moon. Curiously, the conversation did not include Ruth. "It was in my personality to show much more interest in things like this than Ruth," she says. "She seemed not to be interested in the boarding school possibility."

There would be a catch though. Given that Ontario Bible College (OBS) was a private school, there was tuition. Given that it was in Fort Erie, there would be room and board too. The Cressmans could put a bit towards Elsie's education; the rest she'd have to pay herself by working at a part-time job while attending class. Elsie was game for that. She was happier being busy anyway.

As Canada went to war in 1939, Elsie completed her grade nine year at Plattsville Continuation School She counted the days unitl September.

Housed in a formal and elegant Victorian building on the banks of the Niagara River, OBS was a Brethren in Christ-sponsored school.[1] With only seven faculty, four males and three females, for the approximately forty enrolled students, from Grades 9 to 12, OBS prided itself on student success. It's students pursued a Christian-based liberal arts education, with studies in English, History and Mathematics stressed. Music formed the core of extra-curricular activities, although a Ciceronian Literary Society, The Niagara Torch Yearbook and Student Council also thrived.

Elsie quickly found her footing socially at OBS. She roomed with three other students, including her friend Beulah, and relished after-class time with them. A reputation for being a practical joker soon blossomed. She also developed a crush on a classmate, although the relationship didn't advance to boyfriend-girlfriend status. Elsie signed up to work on The Torch, the school yearbook, perhaps a surprising extra-curricular vocation for a young girl who had not fancied herself a literary type. Academics were, as usual, her least favourite aspect of education. "I did just enough work to get by, and remained a very average student." Her favourite subject was Mathematics, and she was good at it.

In recalling her two years at OBS, it was the strictness of the Brethren in Christ religious philosophy which Elsie had the most difficulty assimilating. She explains:

> The Brethren in Christ people were more religious than the Ontario Mennonite Conference that we belonged to. They were more into having revivals, confessing their sins and getting happy about it. Quite frankly, I couldn't stand that part of the school, but I could avoid it and luckily I wasn't the only one who wasn't a Brethren in Christ student at OBS.

She'd had no trouble landing a paying job to support herself at school:

---

[7] *The Niagara Torch Yearbook*, A Student Publication of the Ontario Bible School. (Fort Erie, ON: 1941), 1.

> I worked in the laundry washing linens – sheets, pillow cases and towels. Students had to do their own laundry, but a few boys didn't want to, so they paid me to wash and iron their shirts. I did three shirts for twenty-five cents. I also worked in the kitchen helping to prepare meals and washing up.

The year sped by quickly and happily, and in the blink of an eye it was June. Elsie would not return home. She'd decided to remain behind and look for work in Fort Erie. "Finding a job there was so much easier than around New Hamburg," she offers. And she needed the money desperately. There was a debt she needed to re-pay.

Despite her part-time job, at the end of term, Elsie had found herself $9 in arrears paying her school fees. "I loved to shop," she admits. She'd been left in charge of the last tidying-up tasks of The Torch, and made the decision to borrow the money from the yearbook bank account to settle up her fees. "Just until I got a job and could pay it back." Luckily, employment was not long in coming. She got a job in the cleaning department of the Fort Erie Hospital, washing walls, beds, floors and bedpans. "The first thing I did with my pay was put the money back into the yearbook account," Elsie says.

When a better-paying job appeared as a housemaid for an affluent family in Fort Erie, Elsie jumped. For $11 a week, with her own room and afternoons off to do what she pleased, Elsie cooked and cleaned and carried out whatever other household tasks her employers requested. "So every afternoon I went to the beach which was close to my employers' home," she says, with a smile. By the time school rolled around in September she'd saved a nice nest egg too for tuition, freeing her from her role as boys' shirt laundress. "I had a real nice tan too," she laughs.

Chapter Six
A Natural at Nursing School

St. Mary's Catholic Hospital in Kitchener had developed a strong community reputation with respect to the care it gave its patients, and the quality of the nursing students it graduated each year. In 1941 Elsie joined ten other freshman students in pursuit of their diploma.

Elsie recalls the black and white-clad nuns or teaching sisters, as they were then called as "strict and fussy." "They hovered around us like bees around flowers," she recalls, with a laugh.

There was little sweetness involved though if a student nurse made a mistake. Among the worst was dropping a medical instrument. "You dropped something and it broke, it came out of your pocket," says Elsie. Ruth,[1] who was in the nursing class ahead of her had butterfingers one day and had to pay for a dozen or more broken thermometers at $1 each. "It took her months to pay for them," Elsie reports.

Nursing instruction was split between lectures and practical work. Elsie tolerated the former and shone at the latter.

> I developed a reputation for being a methodical student nurse who would take the time needed with my patients. I never rushed through, like many of my classmates did, but would slowly and carefully do my work, and always stop to talk to the patients.

She recalls the first hospital bath which she gave:

> Of course it was a man, and I was by myself. The man was a character and really laid it on, as he knew how nervous I was. When the bath was over one of the sisters came in

[1] At the time, girls who had completed Grade 11, with acceptable marks, especially in the Sciences were admitted to the two-year Nursing program at Ontario hospitals, including St. Mary's in Kitchener. Ruth Cressman had returned to school, taking this route.

> and asked him how the bath had been. "The best I ever had," the man said, grinning.

Elsie became a favourite of patients, although perhaps not always of the efficiency-minded nursing sisters. Still she garnered respect, as much for her Mennonite background as for her work habits.

> One day, I was by myself, washing off food trays and a sister came in complaining that anther student nurse's belongings had been recently stolen. "The only people you can really trust around here are the Mennonites," she said.

Elsie quickly found her niche in the maternity ward and in obstetrics. She loved the babies and intuitively felt good about helping young mothers bring a new life into the world. "Nothing made me happier then seeing young mothers happy," she says. Memories of her own mother's miscarriages and stillborn stayed with her, and highly influenced her attitude towards life – and death.

> The death of Mother's infants had made her so sad, and they became a negative influence in her life from that point on. The losses made an impression on me too. I think that was why I always did everything that I could to make a mother's birth experience the best possible for her.

Elsie's preferences showed, and before long staff in both departments were asking for her to be assigned to them. With a laugh, Elsie recalls one day working on a medical floor (and not enjoying her shift), when a classmate appeared at her side. The girl indicated that Elsie needed to report to obstetrics.

> Apparently my classmate had been assigned to obstetrics and was not doing a very good job. So the nurses sent her down to find me to come up to take her place. She would take mine on medical. So we were both happy!

She looked forward to feeding, dressing and bathing the infants and her calm nature seemed to have a sedating effect on them. Once, as Elsie was getting ready to leave a shift, she stopped in front of the glass window of the nursery. Inside, a line of bassinettes each held a peacefully sleeping infant. "I must have had a smile on my face as I looked at them, because a sister who was passing by stopped and said to me: "that's what a good nurse does, and you will make a fine nurse."

Elsie was also drawn to the childbirth process, and she gleaned everything that she could from observing this miracle of life. An early influence was a female physician who had the skill of delivering breech babies. Elsie notes that most doctors delivered breeches by Cesarean section. This physician was a rarity.

> She was so patient and worked ever so slowly with the woman and the infant so that the patient could have the natural delivery she wanted. No cutting, no horrible forceps, no episiotomy. It took a long time as compared to a Cesarean, but it was so satisfying to everyone.

She remembers thinking at the time: "so if this doctor can do it this way why can't all of them do it?"

Given Elsie's strong feelings for babies and her joy towards the process of childbirth, one might wonder why marriage, eventual pregnancy and children were not high on her list of life wishes. She answers the question:

> Marriage never really crossed my mind. But then I was a very firm believer in God's guidance. If God decided that my path in life was to marry and have children, then it would happen. If He decided my road in life was a different direction, then so be that too.

Happy and fulfilled in her career path and personal life, Elsie Cressman had little cause to mourn the absence of a steady boyfriend.

Elsie loved adventure and could usually count on her friend Beulah Snyder to be thinking along the same lines. During her second year of nursing school she asked Beulah, now studying at Teachers' College,[1] if she'd like to take a bike adventure—an extremely long one.

> I thought it would be fun to ride our bikes back to OBS in Fort Erie and attend the fall Commencement exercises there. Neither of us had classes on Friday, so we could leave in the morning and be in Fort Erie by mid-afternoon. Then we'd return on Sunday after church services to come back.

Beulah agreed to the caper. "Most other people we told thought we were crazy," Elsie chuckles.

Wearing the requisite conservative Mennonite print dresses and Oxford shoes, our adventurers set off at sunrise. By lunch they stopped to rest near Dundas, taking a break again when they reached Niagara Falls. There they wrote and mailed postcards to friends back home. "We made sure we sent them to people who'd laughed at us and said we'd never get there." By late afternoon, they arrived at the school, tired, sweaty, muscles "zinging" from the work, but none the worse for wear.

When Sunday dawned, the trip home loomed larger than the first leg had two days before. "So we decided to store the bikes at the school and hitchhike home," Elsie reports. And so they did. The sight of two Mennonite girls with their thumbs out was a novel one, and only a few cars passed before one stopped to give them a lift. "We got one ride to Niagara Falls and another one to Galt, where Beulah's Dad came to pick us up," Elsie volunteers.

Elsie was delighted when, the next Sunday, at church a woman who had been one of the trip's chief detractors came up to her to give her congratulations. "I'd sent a post card to her with the hymn 'Rock of Ages' on it," Elsie laughs. "She was now my biggest fan."

---

[1] Elsie did not graduate from OBC, having left after Grade 11 to go into nursing. Beulah, having graduated from OBS the next year was now a student at Teacher's College.

Part Two

A Working Girl

Chapter Seven
First Nursing Jobs

Elsie's formal nursing training ended in the spring of 1946. She would now have a period of work experience before she wrote her final exams. She had full faith that God would determine where her nursing path would lead her.

Her first stint of paid work was as a private duty nurse for a New Dundee area family. The man of the house had had a heart attack and was to be cared for at home. Elsie's job would be to bathe, feed and administer medications to him. The man progressed under Elsie's care, and encouraged by this positive sign, his wife opened the doors to visitors. This tragically spelled the man's death. Elsie explains:

His heart was still so weak and he needed complete quiet. But his wife gave in to the friends and relatives who wanted to visit him. When I left to go home one evening, there were too many people there and I knew it was not a good situation. He died later that night.

One or two other private duty short-term nursing jobs followed before Elsie tried her final exams. She "just passed," but now Miss Elsie Cressman could add "RN" after her name. She could also divest herself of the despised student nurse aprons and bibs, in favour of crisp nurse's whites and banded cap.

Elsie describes her nursing style as she was about to embark on her career:

> I was a cautious nurse, always concerned about making a mistake. That made me rather methodical and somewhat slow in my work. Patients seemed to like this approach though. I guess my supervisors were OK with it too. I got along well with them and with my fellow nurses too.
>
> Even though I was somewhat uncertain, especially at the beginning, I was a real stickler for rules. If a rule was

there, even something like visitors respecting visitation times, I made sure it was enforced.

Registered nurses could follow two paths to employment in those days. They could work in a public setting such as a doctor's office or hospital, or they could do private duty work. The latter might be in the patient's own home, or giving extra care and attention to one in the hospital. There were pros and cons to both choices. Private duty nurses earned more than those working in a public setting, but the work was less challenging. "Much of the time it was more like babysitting than anything," Elsie indicates.

At the bottom of her financial barrel after three years of school, Elsie initially opted for a private duty nursing stint at St. Mary's Hospital. Her patient would be none other than Kitchener socialite Roxy Lang, matron of the wealthy Lang family. Mrs. Lang was recovering from an operation, and as a "VIP," she would not be expected to share nursing staff with lesser souls. Elsie remembers Mrs. Lang:

> Well the first thing I remember is that she wore ladies' gloves, but wore two different colours on her hands. I guess this was fashionable. She also had more flowers than any other patient I had ever seen. It was my first job each day when I arrived to dump out the old flowers and arrange the new ones that kept coming. I'd then give Mrs. Lang her breakfast and a bath.

She recalls that when one nursing sister learned that Elsie Cressman, a Mennonite farm girl would be the society maven's private nurse, the sister questioned the suitability of the placement. "But Mrs. Lang told the sister that I was 'just fine,'" she laughs. For much of the time as Roxy Lang's private nurse, she read or knitted beside her patient's bed.

A short stint as a general duty nurse working nights in the nursery at St. Mary's followed. A particular baby was sickly and she spent extra time at his side. One night at the end of her shift when Elsie reported to the night nurse, she noted that the infant seemed poorly and was slow to wake up. She hoped he would improve after a dose of his midnight medicine.

The next day when Elsie returned to work, she was horrified to learn that the infant had passed away during the night. Her anger deepened when it was uncovered that the night nurse had neglected to medicate him. The experience shook Elsie deeply.

> Babies were so special and this one was more so, being sick. And he had died because someone hadn't done her job. It upset me terribly and I reported what I knew to the supervisor. But nothing was done. The sick baby was dead and that was it.

Elsie was now ready to move on to richer learning experiences than wealthy ladies with different coloured gloves. A position in the Mennonite Hospital in La Junta, Colorado had come up and she meant to take it.

La Junta had a large Mennonite population. At the turn of the century a number of Mennonite farmers from the American mid-west had settled in this fertile area in southeastern Colorado and began farming. Soon afterwards, they established Colorado's first Mennonite Church.

In 1920, the city fathers of La Junta asked the Mennonite community to take over the administration and running of the La Junta Hospital.[1] Mennonite efficiency and productivity was well-known and respected in La Junta, as it was (and remains today) throughout North America. The La Junta Mennonites acquiesced to the request, and ran the facility until 1927.

During that time, they built a new hospital and a tuberculosis sanitarium. The sanitarium's reputation soon passed beyond the state to international recognition. Each year hundreds of tuberculosis

[1] Bender, Harold S. "La Junta Mennonite Hospital (La Junta, Colorado)" Global Anabaptist Mennonite Encyclopedia Online. n.d.,www.gameo.org.

patients traveled to the dry mountain air of the state to seek treatment at La Junta. At the time those afflicted with the often fatal disease were housed in isolation in the sanitarium, apart from the hospital.

It was at the La Junta Hospital where young Elsie Cressman set her sights. Soon after her St. Mary's graduation, she made written application to the hospital. She didn't have to wait long for a reply. La Junta was pleased to offer her employment. But given visa restrictions, the position could only be for six-month's duration. No problem for this optimist. She looked forward to learning what she could in that time.

Hearing through the grapevine that someone was driving to the state of Kansas, she hitched a ride. This would also give her the opportunity to visit her sister Ruth, who was now working as a midwife in rural Arkansas. After graduating from St. Mary's Nursing School, Ruth had attended Goshen Mennonite College in Indiana. She then took midwife training with famed American midwife Mary Breckinridge. Midwives in the practice targeted isolated and often illiterate women living in the Appalachian and Ozark Mountain regions of Arkansas, Tennessee and Missouri. They often visited their clients on horseback. Elsie comments on the unlikely direction that her reserved sister followed in her life:

> Ruth was studious, feminine and quiet, while I was noisy and a tomboy. Ruth was the good daughter; I was the bad one! She did housework inside; I did farm work outside. Ruth usually hung back and took the safe way in most experiences, while I was the one that pushed and wanted to try to new things. It was surprising that she became what she did.

Still, the two sisters were close. Elsie looked up to her older sister and followed her advice.

Chapter Eight
La Junta, Colorado

In thinking back on her six months at La Junta, Elsie says: "My time here was short, but the experiences that I had carried over to the rest of my life." Her position would see her working initially as a general duty nurse on one of the hospital's medical floors. But once her interest and expertise in obstetrics and the nursery were uncovered by hospital staff, she found herself stationed in these two wards. Within weeks of arriving, she was acting as night supervisor in obstetrics.

Delivering mothers were routinely given chloroform. Discovered in 1847 and lauded as an effective anesthetic, chloroform reached the height of its popularity when it was used to sedate Queen Victoria[1] during the delivery of her ninth child, Princess Beatrice. So delighted was another Victorian society matron with her so-called "painless childbirth" under the effect of the gas, that she named her child Anaesthesia!

Elsie saw first-hand the drug's benefits to the medical professionals in the delivery room, and its drawbacks for the delivering mother. It was administered by placing several drops on a facemask which then covered the mouth and nose of the patient, chloroform acted immediately by depressing the central nervous system, thus inducing unconsciousness. While still conscious, the woman remained sedated and felt little pain.

Still, chloroform was a potentially lethal drug. Cases of immediate cardiac arrest had been reported by various hospitals and by the 1930's it had fallen out of favour. Ether was now the anesthetic of choice in many maternity wards. There were problems with this sedative too. Ether was highly flammable and an irritant to the eyes; it also caused nausea and dizziness. Both chloroform and ether were replaced in the

[1] "Anesthesia and Queen Victoria," UCLA Department of Epidemiology, School of Public Health. n.d. www.ucla.edu/EPI/snow/vicoria.html.

1950's by the safer anesthetic, hexobarbital.

At St. Mary's, Kitchener, both ether and chloroform, depending on the delivering physician's personal preference were used in births. As a student nurse, she'd viewed both drugs unfavourably.

> But if I'd had a choice, I'd have chosen ether, which was milder than chloroform. Chloroform was potent. Still both were narcotics and dulled the experience of childbirth, for both the mother and the baby. Newborns were groggy out of the womb. Babies born the natural way were brighter and more alert.

Now at La Junta, delivery room physicians liked chloroform, and the more the better, it appeared.

> All the doctors insisted on chloroform, and as delivery room nurse, I was the one who had to administer it. I can still remember the words I heard over and over again from them: "pour on more chloroform, pour on more chloroform!"

She'd observed in both settings that, given their druthers, many women preferred no anesthetic or sedative. "But women didn't know their rights then," Elsie says. "They would do anything the doctor wanted and would never press their own opinions against him—it was usually a him." In a position to use some passive resistance at La Junta, Elsie would hold back on administering the chloroform as long as possible, and would stint on it even when urged by the doctor to "pour it on."

She saw more forceps-assisted births than she cared for too. "Oh forceps were horrible tools," she recalls, "and I hated them. I kept thinking that if doctors weren't in such a hurry and took their time, forceps wouldn't have been needed at all."

These ideas would find a permanent lodging place in Elsie Cressman's brain. They'd form a major part of her own birthing philosophy, decades later.

There was another part of the La Junta complex that existed outside Elsie's daily routine. This was the sanitarium for tuberculosis patients. At the time, tuberculosis was a virulent and often fatal disease and entry into a "san" was often the last step of a losing battle against the disease.

While prognosis for tuberculosis patients had improved since the 18th century, when 25% of all deaths were attributed to TB, by the time Elsie worked in La Junta, there was still no effective cure. Streptomycin, the first antibiotic used to treat tuberculosis was not discovered until 1946. Effective treatment of the disease was not widespread until the late 1950's.

Patients who could afford it, chose the dry mountain air of Colorado for treatment. As a result many sanitariums operated in the region. One of the best was La Junta Mennonite Sanitarium. During Elsie's stay there, care in "the san" meant isolation, healthful food, bed rest and clean air. Experimental treatment saw air injected into the lungs. Attempts were also made to decrease the lung size by means of a procedure called thoracoplasty.

Elsie had had no training or exposure to tuberculosis in her nursing training and she felt out of her depth. When she was asked to do some relief work at the sanitarium, she was at a loss to know how to deal with TB patients. She vowed to expand her nursing knowledge to include the disease. "I'm sure I made some terrible mistakes over my times on the TB ward, and I didn't like feeling that way at all," she confesses.

Free time in La Junta meant trips outside the town to mountain towns such as Aspen and the capital, Denver. In one memorable excursion, she took her first airplane ride to Salt Lake City to meet her parents who were visiting there. The trio then drove back to La Junta so Curtis and Amanda could see where Elsie did her work.

Before she could blink an eye, Elsie's six months' of duty was up. She was heading to Kansas, the next stop along life's journey.

Chapter Nine
Kansas City Mennonite Children's Home

> I never planned ahead and I never worried about what would come up next. I left that up to God. He led me from one place to another and I fully left that up to Him. I'd just follow. I always felt that my life just fell together like it was supposed to.

Such was Elsie Cressman's life philosophy and she borrowed from it liberally throughout her life. God had now led her to the Mennonite Home for Children in Kansas City, Kansas. How long she'd stay there was up to Him.

The Mennonite Children's Home of Kansas City, Kansas had been established in 1917 as a response to the growing number of neglected, abandoned or abused children in need there.[1] Owned and operated by the Mennonite Board of Missions and Charities, the home provided temporary homes for children in foster care or seeking adoptive homes. Approximately forty-five children, ranging in age from two years of age to twelve, lived in the residence. All attended a nearby public school.

Between fifteen and twenty staff cared for the kids in various capacities: child workers, office, kitchen and general household staff. Elsie would fill the key role as the Home's nurse. Her living quarters on the first floor included a bedroom, a treatment/dispensary room, and two small rooms where sick children could be housed on a temporary basis.

With no residential doctor, Elsie's work was cut out for her. She treated various childhood illnesses: flu, colds and chicken pox, as well as tending to cuts, scrapes, bruises and bonks. For a take-charge gal like Elsie, this job was heaven. The children liked her too. With

[1] Yoder, Glen, "Mennonite Children's (Kansas City, Kansas)" Global Anabaptist Encyclopedia Online, 1957. www.gameo.org.

her calm demeanor and cheery outlook, visits to "Nurse" were not dreaded at all.

Surprisingly, the children exhibited few behaviour problems other than childish pranks. With a laugh, Elsie recalls an innocent one:

> Once, a few of the boys escaped down the fire escape and headed back to their own homes. But we alerted the police who rounded them up and returned them to us. And they were happy to be back after a bit of adventure.

Good working conditions and excellent team spirit[2] encouraged staff to go the extra mile for their charges. Often they developed a significant attachment to particular kids. Elsie particularly recalls Donnie, a little boy who she took under her wing for a time. When the youngster was scarcely more than a year old, he had accompanied his mother, a single parent as she hitchhiked from town to town in the central US states. Donnie was a forlorn and bewildered toddler when he ended up in care.

> Donnie was such a cute little guy and I pretty well treated him as my own for the time he was with us. His bedroom was in one of the rooms at the back of my living quarters and I played with him when I was off duty.

One day Donnie's mother showed up again, wanting him back. Elsie was furious.

> I went to court to say he should stay with me but the mother wanted him back and a mother's rights are stronger than a conscientious caregiver. So he left. What ever became of him I never knew. I was so disappointed and missed him greatly.

Socially too, Elsie had immediately felt at home at the Kansas City Mennonite Home for Children, and made fast friends there. She calls herself at age twenty-five, "a high-spirited young woman, who

---

[2] The group of ten Kansas City co-workers continued to correspond by means of a regular newsletter, humorously called the FOM's (Fat Old Maid's), after Elsie left Kansas City. Elsie's letters to Mary King from Africa provided valuable factual information about her years at Shirati Medical Mission.

liked to have fun." These characteristics endeared her to people who were of like minds. Mary King from Iowa, the Home's cook, became a particular friend and the two remained in correspondence long after Elsie moved on from Kansas City.

Up until now, Elsie still hadn't had a serious boyfriend. This changed in Kansas City with Don Bench. Don, a Missouri native, worked at a department store and attended the same Kansas City Mennonite church as Elsie. They began to date.

Social times with Don often took place at concerts and church activities. This would often be followed with Elsie bringing her beau to the Home for dinner. She recalls a practical joke once played on them by a few of her colleagues:

> When we arrived back, Don left his keys in the ignition of the car. People did that all the time then. Nobody would steal a car parked in front of Mennonite Children's Home! When it was time for him to go home, he went out to his car and found the keys gone. He came back in to report and I immediately suspected one of my friends of swiping them. I charged up to her room where several of them were socializing. Their faces told me that my suspicions were true. "Where are Don's keys?" I asked, and when no one volunteered I started to dump out dresser drawers. That produced the keys pretty fast!

Elsie and Don dated for about six months. Then she started to have doubts of his moral character. "He just didn't have the same religious convictions that I had," she says. Religious convictions to young Elsie Cressman meant following – to the letter – the teachings of the Mennonite Church and particularly the Bible. "I wasn't convinced of certain church teachings if they weren't Bible-based," she says. For Elsie to develop strong bonds with those around her, be they colleagues or social friends, they ultimately had to share these beliefs. Not that being religious meant you couldn't have fun.

> I liked having fun and even doing crazy things like practical jokes. But that fun had to be innocent and not

> breaking any rules or Bible teachings – like stealing or other moral teachings. Fun for me had to stay close to those strong Christian values that my parents and my Church and the Bible had taught me.

So when Don's "true colours" began to show, Elsie broke off the relationship. Don Bench would be Elsie's Cressman's one and only serious boyfriend. At age twenty-five, an age when many young women were husband-hunting, Elsie had no fears of remaining an old maid.

> I had thought of marriage but I had no intention of getting involved with anyone who didn't share my beliefs. And even if I had, I really wasn't sure how having a husband would have fit into the way my life was. I wanted a career, and that was more important than having a boyfriend or husband. Staying home and keeping house, which was what married women did at the time, just wasn't an option for me.

By 1949, Elsie was ready to move on to the next stage of her life. She'd had two good work experiences and had been able to save a bit of money. Now the time was right to go back to school and gain a college degree.

Chapter Ten
Back to School

Given her self-assessment that she was a "mediocre student" who did "just enough work to get by," Elsie's decision to attend college might seem a surprising one. Still as a member of a family where both parents and sister had attained their college degrees, perhaps her goal is not as strange as first it appears. Ruth Cressman had completed her nursing certification at St. Mary's Kitchener a year ahead of Elsie. She'd then left for the US to attend her parents' alma mater, Hesston College, before transferring to Goshen College, Indiana. She attained her degree in Science there.

Elsie, individualist to the core, had decided to follow a different route. "There was only one place I wanted to go," she says, "and that was EMC, Eastern Mennonite College in Virginia." She explains her choice simply. "It was a conservative college that fit well into who I was and what I believed in."

Founded as a secondary school in 1917, Eastern Mennonite College (EMC) of Harrisonburg, Virginia had re-invented itself as a two-year junior college by 1947.[1] The campus remained a modest one, with one four-storey building serving as classrooms, a library, a cafeteria and a chapel.

During the Great Depression, EMC had fallen on hard times. Their enrollment dropped to twenty-five students with only six faculty working. But as the economy improved, so did EMC's fortunes. Much of this serendipity was due to former EMC student, one Jacob A. Shenk. Shenk had made his fortune in poultry hatcheries, and put up $20,000

[1] The history of EMC is celebrated in the special 90th Anniversary edition of the student publication *Crossroads* which is available online at www.emu.edu.

seed money to construct an industrial arts building, a chapel and a home economics building on the campus. Thanks to philanthropist Shenk, in 1948, a women's dormitory was also built. Up until this point, women students had rented rooms outside the campus.

Accommodations for male EMC students continued to be spartan, with first-year men housed on the second floor of the Shenk hatchery! Curtains drawn between the individual cubicles were the only form of dorm privacy. Not until 1952, was a new men's dormitory completed.[2]

Elsie was a mature twenty-five years of age, a professional woman, when she began classes at EMC. As such she had some adjusting to do with some of the college's rules for students – most at least five years younger than herself. "Women had to wear long sleeves summer and winter," she says, "and that was pretty silly." She also recalls, with humour, a "kerfuffle" caused among college faculty, when a social event found students tooting on little horns and females decked out in vintage long dresses. "Teachers felt that it was inappropriate for Mennonites to be behaving like this," she says, with a chuckle. "I thought these criticisms went a little too far."

It tested her patience too, needing to submit to such adolescent rules as curfews and restrictions about going off-campus after dark. Fraternizing with teenagers took a bit of adjustment too. "But I never set myself apart from the other students," Elsie states. "I focused on fitting in."

Fitting in, meant letting her mischievous side show. Elsie was not above pulling pranks and playing practical jokes on friends. She recalls an evening stroll with a friend that ended up at EMC's just-completed retreat facility, "Cabin in the Woods." The girls found a car parked outside the building, with a couple enjoying some "alone time"

[2] Today Eastern Mennonite University (previously College), has an enrolment of 1,600 students and focuses its curriculum to "educate students to serve in a global context." The campus, just outside Harrisonburg, Virginia, a small city of 44,000 residents boasts 50 academic buildings set on a campus of 97 acres. www.emu.edu.

in the cabin. This was a perfect occasion for a bit of good-natured trickery, in Elsie's books. "So we ran around and gathered up all sorts of tree branches and sticks and loaded them all in the guy's car," she chuckles. "Then we scurried home". But the hi-jinx had made them late for curfew, and they needed to ring the bell to be allowed in the dorm.

> The Matron scolded us, threatening that we'd be punished. And we were. We were grounded for several days and not allowed to leave campus. It was a bit embarrassing being treated like a child, when I was twenty-six. But I deserved it; I had done a childish thing too.

Then there were the academics. Age had not improved Elsie's love of study. When she'd first arrived on campus, to her surprise, she'd been slotted in as an EMC History major. "I have no idea how that happened," she laughs, "but I stuck with it – lots of reading and lots of essays." Languages were a lost cause too. "I enrolled in a German class and never understood it," she chuckles. She liked Math class, and her survey English course on Shakespeare was surprisingly enjoyable. "I had never read Shakespeare before, and I loved his plays," she recalls. Ironically, considering her later professional direction, Science intimidated her.

> I'd been given credits for Science courses that I took in nursing, but I soon found that I had a very poor grounding in them. So in Biology and other Science courses at EMC I struggled academically, although I passed them in the end – just.

In the warm southern air, classes were often held out of doors. Off-campus field trips, sleeping under the stars of a Virginia sky were magical. "Oh it was beautiful," Elsie recalls.

Keeping up with school work often took second place to earning some much-needed money. Once a week she biked into Harrisonburg to do some night shift nursing at the local hospital. "I always had to work," Elsie explains, "and it helped keep my nursing skills up while I was away from it."

Occasionally she did some part-time work assisting the campus nurse. She recalls a flu epidemic hitting EMC. Her job was to take food trays into the men's dormitory for the bed-ridden students. "Once or twice I barged in to see guys in their underwear or nothing at all," she laughs, "so I soon learned to knock and announce myself," she laughs. "It was especially embarrassing because I knew many of these guys as classmates."

Elsie finished her first year at EMC respectably. Her grades ranged from C's – languages and Science to an A in Shakespeare. She'd be back for Year Two in September, but first she needed to earn some much needed cash. A job as a nursing assistant for a doctor in neighbouring West Virginia came up, so Elsie spent the summer in the hot and sticky South.

Curiosity, more than dissatisfaction got Elsie thinking about switching colleges at the end of her second year at EMC. "I'd heard how liberal and worldly Goshen College was, and I was curious to see what that meant." She hastens to add that she had other reasons to jump the EMC ship too. "I wanted to get a Bachelor of Arts in Nursing Science and I couldn't get that at EMC." Accordingly, she enrolled at Goshen Mennonite College in Goshen, Indiana in September 1952.

Like its Mennonite "cousin," EMC, Goshen had humble beginnings. Founded by the Mennonite Church USA in 1894, Goshen had been born as the Elkhart Institute of Science.[1] In 1903, it moved to nearby Goshen. It was accredited as a complete college in 1908, and awarded its first Bachelor of Arts degree in 1910.

Goshen promoted the Mennonite tenet of stewardship, and in the years leading up to World War I had encouraged its students to choose "Christian service over quiet security" and complete a term of volunteer work overseas.

[1] John S. Umble. "Goshen College (Goshen, Indiana, USA)." Global Anabaptist Mennonite Encyclopedia Online. 1956. www.gameo.org.

Falling victim to philosophic internal turmoil in the early 1920's, college leadership became divided over whether to chart a conservative or liberal course for the future. Goshen closed its doors entirely for the school year 1923-24, while its leaders sorted out their considerable differences. Liberalism emerged the victor and college conservatives split from the institution. Two new conservative Mennonite colleges, EMC and Hesston College were the result.

The 1940's saw Goshen College serving as a "relief training school," readying Mennonite conscientious objectors for service work as an alternative to front line battle. With the war a scant seven years in the past when Elsie Cressman arrived, and tension still brewing in Europe, Goshen remained in relief-training mode.

From her first step onto the campus, Elsie found out what all the talk of "Mennonite liberalism" was about.

> Goshen girls didn't dress the way we had to at EMC. They could wear short-sleeves – a wonderful relief in hot summer weather. Some of the girls didn't even wear head coverings and had their hair cut short. In fact they looked pretty much like college girls at any other college or university in Canada and the United States.

Another shock was the open playing of card games at Goshen. "They weren't playing 'Mennonite cards,' like Famous Authors or Uno either. No. Students here played real cards, with the Queen, King and Jack." Elsie's conservative background had taught her that playing cards was nigh on to consorting with the Devil. "The Bible tells you to avoid playing cards, because this might lead to gambling – a big sin." And while she may not have agreed with some of the activities she saw around the Goshen campus, they didn't cramp her own style. "I did what I was comfortable with, and let others do what they wanted."

Elsie lived off campus and boarded with one of the Goshen professors. She had a roommate, a girl she had never met before. "We had to sleep in a double bed together, but didn't think anything of it. It would have been tough though if we hadn't gotten along."

As had been the case at EMC, Elsie worked part-time as a private duty nurse off-campus The time away from studies didn't do her any favours. "My grades were as they had always been – mediocre," she says. But Elsie wasn't at Goshen to win any academic scholarships. She did need to earn money though to continue her studies. Private duty nursing paid well.

Private duty nurses were much in demand in these dark days, with a polio epidemic spreading like wildfire across Canada and the US. The virulent polio virus not only robbed victims of use of their limbs, but of the capacity to breathe on their own. The most severe of polio victims needed to be placed in an "iron lung" or artificial breathing device. Some improved and could be moved out of the lung when the crisis had passed; others passed months, even years in the metal "coffin." Complications from pneumonia usually caused death.

Elsie cared for several polio victims during her time at Goshen. "I'd open the lung for short periods of time to bathe them or do other personal care, but of course I had to do it quickly and efficiently as they couldn't breathe for long on their own." Elsie recalls one patient who was pregnant when she contracted polio and the baby grew within the lung until it was delivered. So severe was the woman's case, that she needed to return to her breathing shell as soon as the baby drew its first breath. "The baby grew up never knowing what it was to be held by its mother," Elsie recalls.

Having been given credit for her EMC coursework, Elsie completed her Goshen program in the spring of 1953 and graduated with a Bachelor of Arts in Nursing Science. What God might have planned for her next, Elsie did not know, nor worry about. A letter received soon after completing her final examinations, from the Eastern Mennonite Mission Board might point the way.

Chapter Eleven
An Offer She Cannot Refuse

The letter was from a man named Orie Miller.[1] Orie was an important man – the founder and then-current Executive Director of the Mennonite Central Committee. MCC was, and remains today a key player in overseas relief work. He was inviting Elsie to come to Chicago to meet with him to discuss a position at the Shirati Medical Mission in Tarime, Tanganyika. MCC was looking for a strong, independent, self-starter to work at its leprosarium there. Word had passed through the Mennonite grapevine that Elsie Cressman might be the person they were looking for.

> By this time, my father was on many committees in both Canada and the US and was travelling to the US frequently to attend meetings. So I guess you could say that our family had connections. People in the Mennonite Mission Board knew us, and knew about me. This was just a way of checking to make sure that what they thought they knew was the way things really were.

Miller's invitation had only further strengthened Elsie's belief that events in her life were largely guided from "above." "I felt that this was the way it was supposed to be; that I was meant to get this call." Within a week she was in Chicago. The interview went well and Elsie learned that she was the only candidate for the job.

Having passed this "test," Elsie must next submit to a "doctrinal examination" with the Mennonite Missions Board in Salunga, Pennsylvania. The Board would have no interest in her medical credentials, she learned. "What the Board wanted to know was my Biblical knowledge and my personal religious beliefs. I was pretty confident that I was up to par in both areas so I wasn't nervous."

[1] Bender, John M. "Orie O. Miller," Global Anabaptist Mennonite Encyclopedia Online (GAMEO) n.d. www.gameo.org.

In preparation for this meeting, Orie Miller had given her some guidelines.

> He told me to part my hair in the middle, not on the side, the way I usually parted it. I also had to wear a bigger head covering than I was wearing. Of course I must be in a modest dress with a traditional Mennonite cape concealing my bosom. My light stockings needed to be replaced by black ones, and my shoes must be plain and black.

Elsie laughs that these instructions didn't rankle. "I knew that in Africa I could wear my hair the way I usually did, and I could dress the way I wanted as well."

The Pennsylvania meeting went well and Elsie passed the doctrinal examination with flying colours. Much to her delight, as well as the Board's, Elsie found herself employed. She learned that the founder and present man in charge of the leprosarium was Doctor Merle Eshelman. After several years at the helm, he would be returning home to America. Eshelman's shoes were big ones to fill so the person hired to take over must be able to work independently and work hard, as the number of leprosy patients were growing. "It would be a tough job, involving lots of hours and hard work but it was a rewarding position," Elsie recalls with fondness.

The Board had made it clear to Elsie that she'd need to learn Swahili as quickly as possible. Even though most of her patients would be speaking the Luo dialect, Swahili was the second official language of Tanganyika. As an English colony, English was the official language of government, international business and higher education. She'd have to prove her progress in her language instruction too. There was a prize at the end of the journey though. Once Swahili competency was proven, she would have her voice heard in decisions that affected the leprosarium.

Not much intimidated Elsie Cressman. Learning a new language did. "I'd never been good at it, so I knew I'd have my work cut out for me. I'd have to really discipline myself to stick with it." A quick study when it came to hands-on learning, it would have been to Elsie's great advantage if she'd been able to take conversational Swahili classes; even tapes would have been helpful. This bright idea wasn't an option in the early 1950's – mid America. So Elsie's only recourse was book-learning. "I got myself to a bookstore and bought a 'Teach Yourself Swahili' grammar and vocabulary book." By her own admission, she spent little time at it. "It was hard for me so I tended to avoid it."

Elsie would use the time before leaving for Africa to do some medical studying, and this appealed to her. The topic was leprosy. Still, she reckoned her work was cut out for her becoming knowledgeable about society's most despised and feared disease.

The date for Elsie's departure for London, England, the first stop on her journey to Africa had been originally set for December 3, 1954. In mid-November, she received a letter from the Board advising that her departure would be delayed until December 23. They wanted to avail Elsie of the opportunity of traveling with an American missionary family, the Shenks, who had been on furlough for the past year and were now returning to Tanganyika. The Shenks wouldn't be ready to leave for Africa until the later date. "This news disappointed me as I was anxious to get going," Elsie says.

Anticipating her "travel itch", the Mission Board sent her on a field trip for several days' observation at the Carville National Leprosarium located in Carville, Louisiana. Carville was the only such facility in the US[1]

> I learned the basics about the transmission of leprosy and found out it was not contagious in casual contact. Leprosy could only be spread by prolonged skin to skin contact. Even then, some people have a built-in immunity to the disease, no matter what the degree and length of time of skin contact.

[1] Leprosy, its causes, symptoms and treatment are discussed in detail in the Africa section.

Any subconscious fear that she might have had about contracting leprosy was soon dispelled at Carville.

One of the first leprosy patients she met at Carville had lost his nose to the disease. Through him she was made aware of leprosy's social devastation too. Still Elsie was heartened by the progress that was being made in leprosy treatment. Carville was the world centre of medical research into its treatment. Drugs were now available that were showing positive results in halting the replication of the leprae virus and prompting its remission.

> New experimental surgery was also repairing some physical deformities caused by leprosy. There was a doctor at Carville who was doing very early plastic surgery and he could actually stretch their skin to cover places where noses, lips and eyelids had been lost. It was wonderful to learn about this.

The delay gave her time to pay another short visit to her sister Ruth, who was living in Culp, Arkansas, and working as a midwife in a rural clinic. These midwives delivered babies to women living in isolated mountain areas. With few roads, and these often impassable in winter weather, the midwives rode horses to reach their patients.

Ruth had met a farmer named Clifford Strubar who ran an area mission farm. They had become engaged, and planned to marry shortly. The two sisters had seen little of each other over the past few years as their busy lives kept them apart. Little could Elsie have guessed that it would be the last time she would see her beloved Ruth.

Elsie now returned to Pennsylvania, where she was living temporarily, awaiting her departure to Africa. She had expected to see her passport awaiting her, but the mailbox was empty. Elsie was worried. Worry turned to panic when she learned that a postal strike had just begun. No mail was moving and that which had been in transit when the strike began, was stuck inside various post offices across the country. As the days ticked by, with no end in sight to the postal disruption, Elsie feared she'd be staying put.

Two days before her planned departure, she received a phone call from the Mission Board advising her that they'd pull some strings in an attempt to solve the passport problem. But she'd need to leave immediately for New York City, where a representative of the Board would meet her. Enlisting the help of a friend who was willing to be her chauffeur, Elsie set off for the big city. Chatter in the car took her mind off the passport dilemma, but she was bolstered too by her faith. "I knew that I was meant to go to Africa now, and I would sail on the Queen Mary when it left port as planned." Elsie was almost right.

> The Queen Mary was to leave at 10 AM. At that hour, I was still waiting for my passport. I had heard from the Mission Board that the boat would be held only till 2:00 PM for me. You can image the worry I had in those hours! Finally just before 2:00 PM. I got a message that that my passport had been rescued. The US Postal Service had agreed to bend their rules for me.

With that welcome news, Elsie hurried to the pier where the luxury liner was ready to sail. "Within minutes of me boarding the ship, it pulled up anchor and we were off. Imagine that, the Queen Mary waiting for me," she says, with a wide grin.

Part Three

To Africa

Chapter Twelve
On Board Fun

Elsie's traveling companions, Mr. and Mrs. Clyde Shenk and their three children welcomed Elsie on board. She learned that she would be sharing a cabin in the lower steerage area of the luxury liner with the Shenk's twelve-year-old daughter, Mary Catherine. The two sons would bunk with their parents. Always up to any adventure, Elsie had no qualms about bunking in with a child. "How could I complain about anything with the prospect in front of me of spending five days on the world's most famous luxury ocean liner?" Her roommate turned out to be a delightful girl. "Mary Catherine was a real chatterbox and we got on like a house afire," Elsie recalls. The two fast friends passed the time playing games, chatting with other passengers and walking around the deck of the ship. A new shipboard acquaintance was an Englishman who was taking a job in Africa. Elsie thought the man was sweet on her; the suspicion was reinforced when Elsie decided to take a swim in the ship's pool.

> Mary Catherine came rushing in to tell me that she'd overheard the Englishman saying that he was heading for the pool too. In a flash, I got out, dried myself and got dressed. I was self-conscious about my body, and much too modest to be seen in a bathing suit.

Part-way across the ocean, rough seas sent most passengers to buckets and their beds. Elsie and Mary Catherine were miraculously spared the seasickness epidemic, a situation she attributes to them being regular deck-walkers. "People who stayed in their rooms during the storm seemed to be the ones that felt the seasickness most." Dining rooms were virtually empty during the rough weather, but neither Elsie nor her companion missed a meal. Ironically, Elsie felt the effects of five rollicking days at sea after the Queen Mary docked in London.

"The stairs and sidewalks just wouldn't stay still, and I felt pretty woozy for the first couple of days."

Vertigo or no, Elsie was determined to cram as much London sightseeing as possible into her four-day layover. Armed with her trusty 35mm Argus camera she snapped picture after picture of what the great city had to offer tourists – Big Ben, Westminster Abbey, the Tower or London, the changing of the guard at Buckingham Palace, and Madam Tussauds' Waxworks. She recalls the damp, bone-chilling London weather. "I never felt warm for the entire four days we were there." She was itching to get moving into warmer climes.

For Elsie, New Year's Day 1954 must have dawned more portentously than most over the course of her previous 31 years. She boarded the ocean liner M.V. Llangibby Castle of the Union-Castle Mail Steamship Company, and in little more than eight days she would arrive in Africa. There she'd embark on the biggest adventure so far in her young life.

> I always felt that God was leading me, showing me the way in whatever choice I made in my life. And going to Africa was no different. So I felt secure as I moved closer and closer to Africa. I never had any second thoughts or doubts. If I hadn't had that security and trust, I might have felt much different about what was before me.

A surprise awaited the missionaries as they boarded the luxury liner. Expecting the second-class accommodation that they'd had on the Queen Mary, they were surprised to find themselves in first-class passage. The luxury didn't sit right with the plain-living Mennonite missionaries, but there was no alternative. "I guess tourist-class had booked up by the time the Mission Board had made our reservations," Elsie recalls. She rationalized that she would pay her down-to-basics dues once she reached Tanganyika. She relaxed, resigned to enjoying what first-class had to offer. What the ship did offer, for the next day at least, was delay. "Thick London fog kept us sitting in the harbour for over twenty-four hours," Elsie recalls. Finally the pea soup cleared and the Llangibby Castle was on its way.

The steamer would travel down the coast of France and Spain before it entered the warm Mediterranean Sea at the famed Rock of Gibraltar. It would then pass into the Suez Canal at Port Said, travel the length of the canal and exit at the Gulf of Aden. From there it would sail by the "Horn of Africa," plying the coasts of Somalia and Kenya. At Mombasa, East Africa (now Kenya) a large port on the Indian Ocean side of the continent, the ship would put into port, allowing passengers, including the Shenks and Elsie to disembark. It would then complete its journey south to Capetown, South Africa.

Elsie used her time aboard, approximately three weeks, to acquaint herself with her shipmates. Many were heading to East Africa to work. Included in their numbers were teachers, doctors, nurses, agriculture workers and railway officials. Some were higher up the social scale, including a Tanganyikan Chief Magistrate, a District Commissioner, and even a British movie producer. While her conversations with her fellow travelers were interesting and helped her greatly in coming to understand the flavour of the country she would call home over the coming years, it also left her disquieted spiritually. In a letter to friends back home dated February 2, 1954, she was particularly censorious towards non-Christians.

> We were saddened that few of them professed to be Christians and we had to realize that in God's sight they were just as lost as the most primitive Africans. We had opportunities to tell them of the peace and joy which we experience as Christians, and the love of Christ which takes us to Africa. If ever we felt that we were making a sacrifice in going to Africa, I'm sure we felt very much ashamed when we saw the many who were spending their lives in Africa simply for a good position and salary. Surely we cannot think we are making great sacrifices.

The Llangibby Castle's first port-of-call was Gibraltar. The time at dock would allow them to take on crew and supplies and give passengers an opportunity to do a bit of sightseeing. Elsie was eager for the opportunity. "I walked around the entire peninsula taking pictures and seeing the sights." So engrossed was she, that she lost track of the time and arrived at the boat late. "So for the second time an ocean liner had to wait for me!"

Elsie eagerly anticipated her first sight of the famed Suez Canal, the gateway to the African continent. The Canal traced its origins to Ancient Egypt, and historical records speak of canal excavation as early as the 13th century BC. In 1859 Egypt began major reconstruction of the canal and claimed sole ownership. This rankled foreign shipping nations and in 1888 through international agreement, the Suez was declared a neutral zone, open to all nations for transport and commercial trade.

When, in 1895, Egypt claimed to be financially unable to complete work on the canal, ownership passed to Great Britain. Ottoman (Turkish) forces took exception to this action and attacked British troops protecting British interests. The Turks were expeditiously defeated.

Not until 1951 did canal ownership issues resurface. Egyptian Prime Minister Saad Zaghlul declared the Suez to be Egyptian property and demanded that British troops be removed by 1954. It was during this period of "the Changing of the Guard" that the Llangibby Castle, carrying Elsie and the Shenks, entered the Suez. Understandably, the mood aboard all ships entering the canal was tense.

At Port Said, The Llangibby Castle waited for two days in a convoy of ocean-going vessels, waiting to enter the canal. Passengers were free to disembark from the ship in the interim to shop or sightsee. Many, considering the tense political situation elected to stay on board. Not so the intrepid Elsie. With a few other like-minded shipmates, Elsie left for a look-around of the city. It was getting dusk when she finished her tour of the shops. Rather than hiring a guide to take her to the dock, she decided to set off on her own. "I was nervous though, as there were some suspicious-looking characters eyeing me." No doubt the interest was curiosity over criminal. A white woman in a Mennonite head covering and print dress was not the usual tourist.

Elsie passed the rest of the recess on deck playing games with Mary Catherine and other travelers. She even tried her hand at fishing – Mennonite-style. "I put a piece of meat on an open safety pin, attached it to a piece of cord and threw it over the side." Either the fish were used to finer dining or left for cleaner waters than the busy Port Said, because Elsie didn't even get a nibble.

Finally the ship took its place in the convoy leaving for parts south. Elsie recalls the view from the deck of the boat as: "palm trees, camels, low flying airplanes and lots of soldiers." During the ship's succeeding stops, floating trader merchants drew their small boats alongside. Occasionally some would be allowed on board to peddle their wares, but usually business would be conducted over the side of the ship.

> I was talking to a man on board his small boat who wanted to sell me something. He asked me in English, "Are you an American?" I told him "no" and he said: "well what are you?" I didn't see any reason why I should tell him my nationality so I said nothing. Immediately he got this very hateful look on his face and shouted up to me: "You're a Jew." He looked so fierce; I was frightened and immediately moved away.

Anti-Jewish sentiment in Egypt would reach a crisis level two years later, when Egyptian President Nasser closed all Suez shipping to Israeli boats. This provoked the Suez Crisis. Then-Canadian External Affairs Minister Lester B. Pearson, later Canadian Prime Minister would eventually win the Nobel Peace Prize for his work in averting a mid-east war in settling the Suez Crisis. Following Pearson's recommendation, and for the first time in history, a UN-led peacekeeping force was established in the volatile area.

The Llangibby Castle reached the southern end of the Suez Canal and entered the Red Sea. The geography offered a unique experience, affording passengers the sight of two continents simultaneously. To the northeast, lay the desert sands of Saudi Arabia, a part of the continent of Asia; to the southwest, Africa's Egypt, Sudan and Ethiopia.

At the tiny nation of Djibouti, the ship docked. Passengers, among them an ever-enthusiastic Elsie were allowed a brief shore leave to explore its famed market. Elsie and her companion, a South African returning from the coronation of Queen Elizabeth II lost track of time and needed to hurry to catch their "ride." Again, Elsie arrived just as the liner was blowing its "all aboard that's coming aboard" whistle.

Moving now in a more easterly direction, the ship entered the tropical waters of the Indian Ocean. Elsie and her friends were on the home stretch of the adventure. At the bustling city of Mombassa, Kenya, their sea journey ended. A full thirty-three days since she left New York City, a tired but exuberant Elsie, stepped foot onto African soil.

Chapter Thirteen
Wildlife and Mau Maus

Travel now switched from boat to train. At the Mombassa train station, the missionaries boarded a sleeper for the 400 km journey to Nairobi, the Kenyan capital. The journey would take almost twenty-four hours. Elsie recalls her impressions of the compartment that she and the Shenks occupied for the duration of their trip:

> It seemed tiny and very compact compared to those trains I had travelled in at home. We were seated four to a small sitting area, which at night converted to a sleeping compartment. An upper bunk pulled out of the wall and you rented sheets and blankets for the night.

The journey afforded Elsie her first real glimpse of the diverse wildlife that roamed free across the African landscape. She remembers that most passengers, including herself and her faithful companion, Mary Catherine, opened their compartment windows and hung outside. Large herds of grazing Thomson's gazelles, ostriches and other spectacularly-feathered birds were plentiful. Elsie promised herself a trip to Tanganyika's recently-opened Serengeti National Park to see big game such as lions, leopards and cheetahs.

By the time the travelers woke the next morning they were approaching Nairobi, the modern capital of Kenya. There they would have a two-hour wait before transferring to another train for the 350 kilometer journey to Kisumu, Kenya, on the eastern shores of Lake Victoria. After purchasing their tickets, the weary Shenk family sat down in the train station to rest. Elsie decided to take the opportunity to scout out Nairobi.

> The Shenks were horrified when I told them that I was going to walk around town for a bit. They warned me that

> with all the unrest going on with the Mau Mau Rebellion,[1] that it just wasn't safe for a single white woman to be roaming around a big city. But I wasn't worried in the least, and assured them I would be OK – which I was.

Elsie returned safely and this time boarded the train on time. Some additional bodies boarded with her. A number of armed African National Guards stationed themselves at various positions on the train, on the alert against any attacks by Mau Mau extremists on the route. The infamous "Mau Mau Rebellion" was reaching its crisis point just as Elsie was arriving in Africa.

Kenya, with its tropical climate and rich soils, was considered a jewel in Great Britain's colonial crown. Beginning in the 1930's, thousands of transplanted British had taken up residence there. Many became large plantation owners, and grew rich thanks to bountiful crops of coffee, tea, sugar cane and rice. Indigenous African small landowners, primarily belonging of the dominant Kikuyu tribe were pushed off their land to make room for the colonists.

It is estimated that by the early 1940's, over one million Kikuyu tribes people lived in an area no more than 5,200 square kilometers. A population of no more than 30,000 British farmers and their families owned and occupied over 31,000 square kilometers. By the late 1940's, Kikuyu-owned land was almost negligible, and unrest was growing. Over 55,000 British troops were sent to Nairobi and were bolstered by RAF aircraft and the Royal Marines. In March 1953, 1,000 Kikuyu rebels attacked the town of Lari, held by African loyalists to the British crown. Almost 200 of them were killed.

[1] With files from: The Official Kenyan Travel Guide and Travel Information Portal. www.magicankenya.com; The World Fact Book Kenya. www.cia.gov/library/publications/the-world/ke.html; Boddy-Evans, Alistair, "Timeline of the Mau Mau Rebellion. www.africanhistory.about.com/od/Kenya/a/MauMautimeline.html; Slaughter, Barbara, "How Britain Crushed the Mau Mau Rebellion." www.wsws.org/articles/1999/spept1999/mau-s15.shtml

It was in this tension-fraught land that Mennonite missionary nurse Elsie Cressman found herself in January 1954.[2]

Elsie recalls an atmosphere of nervousness, even fear, on the train as the guards stood by. During stops made along the way where passengers disembarked, soldiers followed, rifles at the ready. Such details didn't diminish Elsie's enjoyment of the lush Kenyan countryside and her frequent sightings of wildlife. The train pulled into the Kisumu train station without incident.

Up until this point in her long journey, Elsie's accommodation had been European-comfortable, even to the point of luxuriousness. From Kisumu on, she got her first taste of African bush-style travel. In a January 2, 1954 letter to correspondent Mary King, she describes the journey to the Mennonite Missionary station at Tarime.[3]

> At Kisumu the Shenks and I transferred to an African lorry, or taxi. It was nothing more than a large old truck where benches had been installed for the passengers. In all, thirty-five of us, both native and foreigners, crammed inside. I was later told this was a small crowd compared to other times. And if this is so, I am thankful it was not such a day. It was hot, crowded and sweaty as the truck rumbled along, stopping and letting passengers on and off. Before too long we were thoroughly shaken up and our clothes were brown with the African dust. Still, it was a good way to be introduced to the African style of transportation, and I didn't mind it.

[2] By 1955, Amnesty was declared between rebels and the British government. The bloody battles left over 1 million Kikuyus and Maasai rebels in concentration or containment camps. Thirty-two British and over 20,000 Africans had died in the skirmishes. Kenyan independence was celebrated in 1963, with former Kikuyu warrior Jomo Kenyatta declared President.

[3] At the time, there were countless African Missions, supported and staffed by a wide variety of Christian churches including: Baptist, Roman Catholic, Pentecostal, Seventh Day Adventist, United, Methodist, Anglican. The Eastern Mennonite Board of Missions predominated in the Lake Victoria area.

Elsie had occasion to use her limited Swahili on the truck journey. She glows to Mary in a letter: "I said to the driver, 'Ngojo kidogo,' which means 'wait a minute,' and he understood me! I'm pretty proud of myself." Up until this point, in her frequent letters to friends and family back home, she had made scant reference to her language studies. Indeed in one letter she advises that she'd decided that homework was best kept for less-stimulating times than world travel. Still it appears that this avoidance was causing her some guilt and worry. In another letter she alludes to the sorry state of her language struggles:

> So far I have learned only a few words of the language and I really must dig in now, as I'm almost at Shirati. I will need to spend at least five hours a day on it. I ask you to remember me in your prayers, as I try to learn the language.

Three lorry changes and fourteen hours later, Elsie and the Shenks reached Tarime. It was here that the Shenk children would part from their parents. They were enrolled in the Mennonite-run Marahill Missionary School there, one of approximately thirty missionary schools in the Lake Victoria area of Tanganyika and Kenya. Elsie calls the school "a beautiful building," but notes in a letter that the school children had to use outdoor toilets. Remembering her childhood days on the farm with no indoor plumbing she adds: "but that's not so bad because it's never cold here." Here too Elsie parted with the elder Shenks. They were returning to their positions at Oumangi Mission in the Belgian Congo.

Elsie carried on to nearby Nyabasi Station and a several week respite from her grueling trip. Travelling now for forty-eight hours straight, she collapsed onto the cot put up for her in a station guestroom. She had a "roommate."

> Just as I pulled up the bedcover, I looked down beside the bed and saw a scorpion. I recognized it from a picture I had seen in a book of poisonous insects of Africa. And I knew that I needed to do something about it before I went to sleep. So I quickly popped a drinking glass over

> him and left it there. And I slept like a log for the rest of the night.

Elsie's delay at Nyabasi was one of necessity. The new nurses' residence at Shirati was not yet complete, and presently there was nowhere to house her. The best guess for occupancy of the new four-bedroom dormitory was early February. She chafed at the delay. "I am anxious to get settled," she tells Mary King in a letter dated January 30, 1954, a week after her arrival in Mombassa. Still in Swahili-avoidance mode, Elsie had resolved to use her time at Nyabasi to become acquainted with the missionary and medical work that was going on in this part of East Africa.

On February 5, she received news her Shirati home was complete enough to move in. Excited and eager, she was also fearful. In a February 2 letter she writes:

> I have a huge task ahead of me. One could easily spend five years here and not get a good control of the language which is so essential to understand and work with the people. I long for the time when I can really speak to them. It is certainly not hard to love them. The little babies on their mother's backs are so sweet and all I can say to them is "jombo" which is the equivalent of our "hello."

Chapter Fourteen
The Shirati Medical Mission

The founding of the Shirati Medical Mission is traced back to 1934.[1] In that year, the Mennonite Church of America (Lancaster Mennonite Conference) sent four missionaries, John Jr. and Ruth Mosemann; Elam and and Sarah Stauffer to East Africa. There, two miles from Lake Victoria in the Musoma District of Tanganyika Territory, East Africa, they founded Shirati Mission.

The Mosemanns' and Stauffers' original task was a weighty one. They were to bring the Christian word to Africans and establish a "self-supporting, self-propagating and self-governing Christian (Mennonite) church in the Musoma District." They wasted no time in doing so. A year later, the missionaries celebrated the establishment of the first Mennonite Church in the District. Fifteen Africans were baptized as Christians and six were received into church fellowship.

Elam Stauffer became East Africa's first Mennonite bishop in 1938. He oversaw all Mennonite church and mission work in Africa. Stauffer remained in this position until 1941 when American Ray Wenger arrived to assist. After Wenger's untimely death in 1945, Stauffer carried on alone.

Over the coming years, work and progress continued. By 1950, the Mennonite Church and its missions were a strong presence in East Africa. Five missions had been founded: Shirati, Bukaroba, Mugango, Bumangi and Nyabasi, and workers were placed in Ikoma Mugumu. By the time Elsie arrived four years later, Kisaka, Tarime and Musoma missions had joined the other five. Over 1000 Africans had been

[1] With files from: "A Brief History of Shirati Hospital" from *The Hummels in Africa; AnotherNiftySite.* www.hummelsinafrica.org/article.php?story+20050511131334356; Eshelman, J. Lester and Lois. "Green Grows the Willow." *Shirati Hospital 1935 to 2005 and 1935 to 2007 The Medical Development of Shirati and its International Relationships.* Morgantown Penn: Mastoff Printers, 2007; Stauffer Elam W. and Mahlon M. Hess. "Kanisa la Mennonite Tanzania." Global Anabaptist Mennonite Encyclopedia Online, 1987. www.gameo.org/encyclopedia/contents/K365.html.

baptized into the Mennonite Church.[2]

The mandate of the church to establish a fully African self-governing Mennonite Church was realized in 1966 when Zedekia Kisare was elected as the first native Bishop of the African Mennonite Church.[3] In keeping with this goal, the church adopted the Swahili name, Kanisa la Mennonite Tanzania (KMT).

From its origins, Shirati had been designated as a medical mission, with a commitment to provide education and health care to resident Africans. In 1934, shortly after her arrival, Ruth Mosemann first dispensed medicine to the sick. Her "hospital" was a two-room, grass-roofed hut built by a local tribal chief. By 1936, Dr. Lillian Shenk, Shirati's first surgeon had joined Mosemann and performed the first surgery.

Shirati expansion and progress came rapidly over the next fifteen years. A church was soon erected. Built of white-washed, mud-brick as were most buildings in East Africa, Shirati's house of worship was designed to hold a congregation of almost 300. They'd worship sitting on backless benches of concrete-covered mud brick. Large open windows let in the bright African sunshine. The steeple held a farm bell, which had in earlier times called hands to dinner on a Pennsylvania farm.

The year 1940 saw Shirati's first dispensary open. The building included several small treatment rooms and space to store and dispense medications, splints, bandages and other medical paraphernalia. Without a central residential hospital, patients would remain for their hospital stay in one of ten mud brick, thatch-roofed huts.[4] Each held at

[2] Africans with Mennonite Church membership is estimated at approximately 50,000 in 280 congregations.

[3] Tanganyikan independence was granted in 1961. In 1963, its neighbour Zanzibar was also granted independence and joined with Tanganyika to become the country of Tanzania.

[4] One of these huts held Elsie's patient overseer, as seen in the chapter "Discipline and Values."

least one bed, some two, with a small area for cooking[1] located in one corner. Meals were provided by patients' families.

Five years later, in 1945, construction of a fifty-bed hospital was nearing completion. Built also of burnt brick, the hospital floors were of cement. Two wards held approximately twenty-five to thirty patients each. The building also boasted two operating rooms. The exterior of the hospital featured a large front porch. Frequently families of patients would hold vigil there each night until the patient was released.

By 1948, Shirati's focus had broadened to preventive medicine. Dr. Noah Mack vaccinated over 66,000 Africans for smallpox. The same year, American Dr. Merle Eshleman treated Shirati's first leprosy patients at a location approximately three miles from Shirati. That year, Shirati's maternity ward also opened. There was no nursery. Newborns were placed in a box by their mother's side until discharged.

Shirati construction continued at a quick pace. The year 1949 saw the completion of its new dispensary and the arrival of the hospital's first x-ray equipment. In 1950, the first blood transfusion was administered. Two years later, a fifty-bed expansion of the original hospital was celebrated. A storeroom, laundry, guest house, pump house and morgue followed.

In his book *Green Grows the Willow*, former Shirati Chief of Staff Dr. Lester Eshelman notes that while progress had come in leaps and bounds, in the 1940's and 1950's, the hospital was still lacking in basic items such as sterile surgical gloves, tubing sets, IV equipment and dressing trays.[2]

Most Shirati staff were American; only Elsie and a fellow nurse were Canadian. Regardless of country of origin, all white people were called "Europeans" by the Africans, though few were born on that continent.

The late 1940's saw three single-dwelling residences on the grounds: for the Mission Superintendent, the compound Overseer and the hospital's Senior Nurse. A small shared accommodation for

[1] Food was not served to patients at Shirati. The patient's family was responsible for this.

[2] Eshleman, *Green Grows the Willow*, p. 53.

African hospital workers was also built. Accommodations for other staff followed, as they arrived. By Elsie's arrival in 1954, a nurses' residence had been completed. While small and somewhat "make-shift," Shirati functioned as a comprehensive medical village.

Over the years, the landscape around the hospital compound had also been beautified. It provided an oasis of green against the brown of the bordering scrub land. Hedges of frangipani and ornamental cacti provided boundaries between buildings, and hibiscus, oleander and bougainvillea added colour and fragrance to the Shirati site. Mission staff had also planted large gardens growing cabbages, yams, green beans and lettuce.

On a systems level, Shirati functioned as both a Mennonite mission and a medical facility. A Superintendent of Missions headed the mission; a Chief of Surgery supervised the hospital and its staff.

Although spiritually from the same conservative Mennonite mindset as the Shirati missionaries, Elsie felt more at home with its medical staff. She recalls some personal discomfort in dealing with the former group:

> There was a movement called the East African Revival Movement, which was going on when I first arrived at Shirati. We medical types joked that you could always tell who they were because they were always apologizing and repenting. We also felt they looked down on us as not pious enough – that we should be out getting people saved.

Chapter Fifteen
Daily Life at the Mission

Approximately ten medical staff lived at Shirati when Elsie arrived. Patient needs were high and two physicians were usually, though not always, stationed there. "They always considered themselves lucky when they could get two," Elsie says. In addition to their hospital duties, doctors were on call to the various outlying nursing stations in the District. Surgery was scheduled in the morning hours when electrical power to the hospital was assured. Doctors made hospital rounds three times a week.

Three nurses, (four when Elsie was commandeered to lend a hand), did hospital duty. When there was only one thinly-stretched resident doctor on duty, nursing staff filled that role. Under the nurses worked several African practical or assistant nurses. Some worked in the operating room, others on the wards. In the early days, before a Shirati nursing school was built, they received their training on the job.

Cleaners and other maintenance staff also found employment at the hospital, although there was no central kitchen staff or galley. Patients' families brought their meals and each staff residence came with its personal kitchen staff.

Shirati also provided alternative service requirements for American Mennonite conscientious objectors. In these post-war years, young Americans were subject to the military draft and were called up for military duty. As conscientious objectors or 1W's, Mennonites did non-military alternative service to fulfill their duty to the government.

Two young 1W's, Hershey Lehman and Cris Peifer were invaluable in supervising the construction of Shirati's water pipeline and water storage building. Hershey also worked closely with Elsie at the leprosarium. When his duty requirement was complete, he returned to the US where he completed his college degree. Hershey later returned to Shirati as an Administrator.

In December 1953, when Elsie departed from North America, she left behind a world exploding with new technology. Only remote households in the backwoods of Canada and the US still heated their homes with fire wood or used kerosene for light. In modern homes, running water came from a tap in the kitchen and bathroom. Clothes were speedily washed by machine and pressed thanks to the electric iron. After a day at work or school, a growing number of North American families sat down to enjoy television. The news of the day was heard on the radio.

Shirati Medical Mission was a step backward in time. Just months before Elsie arrived, staff had celebrated the completion of a two-mile pipeline that assured a reliable source of water from nearby Lake Victoria. The water was not chlorinated and susceptible to bacteria forming.

The Shirati Hospital didn't welcome the electrical age until 1954. Before this, Shirati doctors scheduled operations during the daylight hours when the African sun was strong. For nighttime emergencies, light was supplied by a generator run on diesel fuel. Even with the arrival of electricity, light was not reliable. Surgeries were performed in the morning, when there was a better chance that the electric lights were up and running.

One of Elsie's early letters to Mary King notes that the hospital generator had "gone on the fritz again." When this mechanical failure occurred, emergency surgeries carried on by the light of a hand-held flashlight.

Houses and other buildings in the compound were still lit by kerosene lamps until 1958 or 1959. One of Elsie's letters to Mary asks her friend to mail strainers for the "dirty kerosene" used in their kerosene lamps.

Even when telephones were installed in the late 1950's, they were only for communication within the compound. Telephone contact to the outside came later.

Transportation also remained "in the dark ages." A dirt road connected buildings within the compound and to the leprosarium, three miles distant. In the rainy season, the road was virtually impassable and was often washed away.

Given these conditions, there were few cars on the road. A more common sight were small motorbikes called piki-pikis. The road was also shared with various domestic and wild animals. In an October, 1954 letter, Elsie describes some perils of travelling:

> It is quite an art to drive a car or bike without running over cows and goats. They sure think they have the right of way. I have to get off my bike so I don't run into them. The other morning we were driving to the leper plot and a small goat stuck his head under the wheel of the car. We were going so slow that when we stopped, the front wheel was on his head.

Shirati Hospital's four nurses resided in a four-bedroom burnt-brick house at the extreme south end of the compound, amidst an orchard of mango, orange, grapefruit and papaya trees. Goats and cattle roamed freely outside the yard. Facing northwest, with a view of beautiful Lake Victoria, some two miles distant, the home's front porch afforded the sitter a welcome lake breeze during the stifling African day.

A single bed with mosquito netting was the focal point of each bedroom. A bedside table, chair and stool completed the picture. Elsie's frustration with the housing situation shows in one of her letters:

> We're always bugging hospital administration for furniture such as a desk and wardrobe. But it's like pulling hens' teeth to get them. These men seem to think single girls can live in a little room and turn a box on its side for a dresser. The married couples must have everything. But

> I guess it is not just in the missionary field that single girls get pushed around.

In her autobiography, *Journey Through Time,* nurse Alta Weber, who was at Shirati during Elsie's early years describes how she worked around the lack of drawer and shelf space. "By my bedside I'd placed a fairly large wooden box with wood strips nailed on for standing support. It had an open front, and no drawers. It served its purpose in a so-so way."[1]

Appliances were in short supply too. Elsie complains: "it's impossible to find an iron and even harder to find a place to wash your clothes." She chuckles at the memory of the small refrigerator in the nurse's dormitory. "The fridge didn't work more than it worked, and the ants get into it too."

The nurses entertained visitors while sitting on wooden boxes in the living room. They reserved the "good" seats," a couple of worn easy chairs, two outside porch chairs and an African stool, for the guests. Several pressure lamps provided dim evening lighting. A photo of a seagoing vessel from an old calendar served as the room's only decoration.

In each of the two tiny bathrooms, lake water trickled out of the taps unheated and unpurified. Like most Shirati staff, Elsie soon found it was easier to bathe in the tepid waters of Lake Victoria.

Medical staff was not expected to do their own laundry or keep house or cook. African workers were employed for these jobs.

[1] Weaver, Alta B. *Journey Through Time.* (Ephrata, PA: Grace Press Inc., 2008), 273.

Chapter Sixteen
Dining Shirati Style

Elsie's sense of adventure extended to food and she eagerly sampled African cuisine. She thought considerably less of the kitchen staff who were assigned to prepare meals for the Nurses' Residence. She writes in a letter home:

> If you are ever inclined to think of us living in luxury with native boys to do our cooking and cleaning you can be assured that you have the wrong slant to your thinking. This month has been especially trying. Our cook came late so often that I sent him back home one evening without letting him do his work. He never returned. Our next cook was a boy of twelve – a very loveable little fellow with the cutest giggle. But you can imagine how this is working out. He's lived in a mud hut all his life where they probably only had one pan in their "kitchen."

With no grocery store close to the compound, Shirati relied on locally-grown food, as well as wild game. One dish that Elsie came to enjoy was the grain ugali, a staple in the local diet. Preparation began with the cook hand-pounding it till it resembled corn meal. Then, it was stirred into boiling water until thick. Elsie outlines the next steps of serving the dish:

> The ugali was now placed on a platter or in small bowls. You'd take a fair-sized pinch of it, roll it into a small ball, make an indentation with your thumb and then dip it into a bowl of meat broth. Then you ate it from your thumb. It was tricky at first but once you learned the technique, you enjoyed eating it.

Shirati cooks also baked a sweet potato flour and flake yeast bread which she enjoyed. Samosas were another tasty dish. This spicy main course saw vegetables and goat or pork packed into cornbread pockets then fried or baked.

In the tropical climate, mangoes, guavas, oranges, pineapples and tangerines grew abundantly. Several guava trees also grew inside the Shirati compound and Elsie recalls picking a trailer-full of the treat and delivering it to a nearby boy's school. One letter home describes a special treat – cooked bananas. "They're cooked in skins, mashed like applesauce and made into banana dumplings. I couldn't tell they weren't apples."

Vegetables grew abundantly in the rich tropical soil, and the Shirati gardens overflowed with lettuce, endive, cucumbers, squash, spinach, turnip, radish, corn and tomatoes. Peanuts also grew well. But mudslides could wipe out a season's work in the blink of an eye. And if not regularly watered in the long dry season, tender plants would also wither and die. With no freezing facilities, African cooking staff canned vegetables for use when little fresh food was available.

Elsie's letters give details of other African treats. Pumpkin blossoms were dipped in egg and bread crumbs, then fried. "Delicious," was her verdict. Another adventure was flying white ants. Elsie calls them a "delicacy:"

> These ants are about the size of a Canadian June bug, with a softer shell, but they have wings. After they hatched the cook would pull the wings off while the insects are still alive, put them in a frying pan while they're still moving, and fry until the shell is crunchy. They're tasty, but you have to pick the legs out of your teeth with a toothpick.

Meat, the staple of the North American diet, had a less prominent place on the African table. Geese and ducks visited nearby Lake Victoria during rainy season and were abundant, but domestic cattle, pigs and chickens were only slaughtered for very special occasions. Africans relied more on big game to supply meat for the table. Zebra, topi, impala and wildebeest were plentiful in the area. From time to time, Elsie would have a role in putting wild game on the supper table.

Growing up on a farm, Elsie was handy with a rifle. Her brother Howard had taught her to use a .22 rifle.

> Dad gave Howard one cent a piece for shooting nuisance groundhogs, sparrows and barn rodents. Well, I didn't think that fair at all. I wanted in on the action and begged Howard to teach me. He agreed and said when I could hit a target he'd give me my own supply of bullets.

Little did she think this skill would, one day, make her a bit of a "legend" at a medical mission in Africa!

Chapter Seventeen
Elsie the Sharp-Shooter

Soon after her arrival at Shirati, Elsie had bought a high-powered German Mauser rifle from a departing missionary. She was now well-equipped for any adventure that might come along. But she'd need to do some target practice first with her new gun – a much more powerful weapon than what she'd handled on the farm.

> So I asked my friend Hershey Leaman to take me target shooting. I told him I'd shot a gun before and he said to me, looking at the monster I had in my hands: 'but not one big enough to shoot a buffalo!'

Elsie learned exactly what Hershey was talking about when she took her first practice shot. "The force of the blast threw my shoulder right back hard," she recollects. "It was a bit of a shock." It took some practice, but eventually Elsie became quite a sharp-shooter. Whenever she saw a group of men heading out with rifles slung over their backs, she begged to come along. Skeptical at first, the hunters soon learned to respect her abilities.

Elsie's letters back home after big game hunting trips show her delight of being in the thick of the action.

> We came across a wild pig – the choicest of all meats. Usually one never gets a decent shot at a pig, for they disappear into grass with just their tail showing. But this one was right in front of us and just stood and stared.
>
> Hershey aimed quickly and shot. The pig was gone. I started circling around through the grass and thorn bushes to get back on the trail and behold, we came across our pig kicking its last. It was a huge one, the biggest one we'd ever seen. We headed home with dinner.

Wild animals, attracted by the food at the Shirati compound came to call too. Some caused no alarm; others were more dangerous or destructive. The lumbering hippopotamus fit into the latter category. A large number of the usually-docile beasts called Lake Victoria home. As long as they stayed in the water they caused no problems.

But once the two-ton behemoths, with their massive feet stepped onto land, there was potential for trouble. Hippos loved vegetables, especially cabbages, and would head for the Shirati gardens to root them up. Those that weren't eaten were crushed underfoot. "One step, and two cabbages would be squashed," Elsie reports.

As a result, hippos were not popular around any settlements where produce was grown. Unfortunately for them too, their meat was tasty. Elsie recalls "The Shirati Great Hippo Hunt" that took place shortly after her arrival:

> There was one hippo who'd been making a mess of our garden. It had been spotted in the gardens and shooed away dozens of times. Drs. Yoder, Weber and myself – the only ones who had guns powerful enough to bring down a hippo down – decided that we had to do something soon.

The plan for the hippo's demise (and the mission's dinner) called for the hunters to wait until the beast had re-entered the water after a foray into the garden. Elsie explains why:

> We'd stand a better chance of cashing in on the meat if we shot it when it headed back home to the lake after raiding the garden. If we shot it on land, it would crash into the thick underbrush and disappear. We'd never find it then.

Awakened one night by Shirati's overseer, Elsie was informed that she better get dressed fast and bring her gun. The hippo was in the garden. She met the two other members of the posse at the edge of the lake and waited.

Within minutes they heard a telltale thrashing nearby, and knew the hippo was headed back home with a full tummy. As soon as the animal put all four feet in the water, they'd aim and fire. One bullet alone would probably not pierce the animal's thick leathery skin. However a sure shot in the beast's vulnerable eye or ear would do the damage. Easier said than done, in the dark of a Tanganyikan night!

> We each fired at least three shots but couldn't be sure what part of the body we were hitting, or even if we were even striking the body. We heard a lot of bellowing and splashing and so got the idea that some damage had been done. In the distance we heard the overseer's shout announcing that he thought we'd hit the mark.

A hippopotamus killed in the water will sink for several hours before rising. So the assassin-squad returned to their beds to salvage as much sleep as remained before the sun came up.

In the morning, news of the success had spread through the compound. When reports came that there was a dead hippo floating several feet off shore, a crowd gathered. Several Africans waded into the water to attempt the salvage chore. Given the mammoth size of the carcass, this would be no easy feat.

What the shore party could not see from their vantage point was that a thief had beaten them to the punch. One of the hippo's legs had been removed, with the thief no doubt then returning to his home with meat for the next few days.

Hours later the three-legged hippo was finally brought to shore. A truck and trailer was waiting and the carcass was shoved and lifted on board. "The load was so heavy it tipped the trailer into the air," Elsie recalls, with a laugh.

Eventually, the carcass was decapitated and the body transported to a nearby kitchen. There the thick hide was cut off and the meat was made into steaks, roasts, and the tougher cuts for stews and soups. Even the discarded jawbone had a use. Elsie explains the practice:

> The head was buried and any meat left on the jawbone would rot. The teeth would eventually fall out and be retrieved. Hippo teeth are like ivory, large and very, very hard, and Africans carve them for jewelry.

Elsie eventually inherited the teeth and kept them dear as a memento of The Great Hippo Hunt. The event proved fodder for good-natured fun for weeks afterward. She laughs at the memory:

> Yoder and Weber and I argued about whose gun had brought the hippo down. Yoder's bullets were snub-nosed which would have just sloughed off the hide. Weber was not a very good shot and I'd say to him: "I don't think there was any way you could have aimed crooked enough to hit even something as big as that hippo!"

In the end, most people agreed that Elsie had brought the beast down. "I was a better shot, my gun was bigger and my bullets were hard-nosed," she laughs. Elsie later happily refers to the hippo hunt in a letter to Mary: "I'm sure hippo hunting would go a long way to fixing up your ills. It does mine."

Less intrusive than the hippo, less aggressive than the monkey, but considerably more dangerous, was the African snake. Several varieties of poisonous or constricting snakes lived around the shores of Lake Victoria, including the python. Elsie soon learned to keep her eyes sharp for reptiles.

> Most African snakes are deadly. Some could kill you in an hour. So you quickly learned where they lived, where they liked to sun themselves, and where they looked for food. You wanted to avoid running into them in any of those places.

But if a person did have the opportunity of killing a snake, some varieties roasted were considered a delicacy. Other snakes were killed for their skin; still others just to rid an area of potential danger. One day Elsie had an opportunity to see what she preferred.

> A python had been seen on the porch of one of the guest cottages. It was startled when someone came along and

> it disappeared into a hole at the back of one of the steps. I sure didn't want one of the children coming across it, so I decided to wait until it showed itself again and I'd shoot it.

Trusty Mauser cocked, Elsie sat silently and patiently and waited for the snake to show its cold, beady, black eyes. After some time, she was rewarded and the serpent emerged. "I aimed, fired and shot it right in two," Elsie offers. She gave the skin to one of the Africans to make keepsake for her.

Several varieties of African wild monkeys lived around the Shirati compound, including the "Einsteins" of the monkey world, the baboon. Smaller than hippos, and less deadly than an African snake, a large monkey population could still wreak considerable damage.

> Africans don't think of wild monkeys as cute or funny. They're real pests and can be very aggressive to humans. Baboons are especially bold and will chase people. You run fast when you've got a ferocious baboon with very sharp teeth chasing you down.

One day, seated on the high rocks overlooking the leprosarium, teaching a Sunday School class, Elsie spied a baboon taking an unusual interest in one of the buildings down below. "What is that monkey looking at so intently?" she wondered to herself. Before she could answer, the monkey sprang off the rock toward the closed window of one of the rooms.

It hit the glass, smashed it, and as quick as a wink was inside. The startled class watched in fascination, wondering what could have provoked such unusual (even for baboon standards) behaviour. Within seconds they had their answer.

The beast vaulted through the window, head bleeding but protectively clutching a bunch of bananas. "Other than shock at what we'd just seen, my main feeling was anger at myself for having forgotten to bring my rifle along," Elsie reports.

Baboons also made a habit of terrorizing women tending the compound's gardens. "They'd come pelting down one of the rows of vegetables and the terrified gardeners would run away," Elsie remembers. "The next time you see them," she ordered the women, "come and get me, and I'll grab my gun."

Her chance came the next day, but as soon as the monkeys saw the gun they hi-tailed it to some high rocks. Undeterred, Elsie sat down to wait.

> I didn't have much time to wait. First one, then two, then three heads soon popped up over the crest of the rock face and when they did I was ready. "Pow! Pow! Pow!" I got off three shots and three heads disappeared.

Not until the carcasses of two dead monkeys were brought to her later in the day, and the later report that a wounded one had been found was Elsie convinced she had rid the compound of at least three of the interlopers. "But that was not the end of the baboons," she advises. "There were dozens of them and they had little fear of humans."

CHAPTER EIGHTEEN
The Scourge of Leprosy

After settling in at her residence, Elsie was anxious to get to work at her leprosarium. And thanks to her time at Carville before her departure from North America, she knew a fair bit about one of the world's oldest and most feared diseases.[1]

The nature of leprosy still baffles medical experts. *Mycobacterium leprae,* the bacteria that causes leprosy are usually transmitted between an infected and uninfected individual by close and prolonged skin to skin contact. The bacilli may also enter the body through the nose or though cuts or sores in the skin. Yet, under these same conditions some individuals seem resistant to the disease, and no infection occurs, despite prolonged contact.

Leprosy finds an optimal environment in settings where individuals sleep in the same bed and with bare skin exposed – namely in poor and undeveloped nations.

Not until the late 1940's was there effective treatment for leprosy. It came in the form of the drug Dapsone and once Dapsone was readily available for treatment, dispensaries were soon opened to receive patients. Leprosy treatment was simple too – twice-weekly Dapsone pills. The less severe Tubercular Leprosy patients responded fastest to treatment, with the distinctive copper-coloured spots fading and eventually disappearing. The large skin lesions on the more severe Lepromatus Leprosy sufferers began to shrink too with Dapsone treatment, although total recovery could take up to two years.

[1] With files from: "History of Leprosy." www.stanford.edu/class/humbio103/parasites2005/Leprosy/history.htm; "Leprosy: Hansen's Disease," www.bilkent.edu.tr; "Leprosy." www.nlm.nih.gov/medlineplus/encyc/article/001347htm.

Still the drug performed no miracles. Nerve damage and loss of limbs could not be reversed. While the active disease was now halted, those disfigured by leprosy remained disfigured.

Today, the World Health Organization names nine countries where leprosy is still a public health concern: Angola, Brazil, Central African Republic, Democratic Republic of Congo, India, Madagascar, Mozambique, Nepal, and the United Republic of Tanzania.

Leprosy is rare in industrialized North America and Europe, yet clinically it knows no borders. Given an ideal environment, all forms of the disease can develop and spread in any nation on earth. Despite this discouraging situation, medical experts hope for an eventual eradication of the disease. WHO statistics show 286,000 people diagnosed with leprosy in 2004. This figure is down from 805,000 in 1995. US statistics for 2005 listed 6,500 active cases if leprosy in that nation. 90% of those infected were recent immigrants from countries where the disease is still endemic. Approximately 200 new leprosy cases are identified in the US each year.

At Shirati Medical Mission, Dr. Merle Eshelman joyously heard the news of the long-awaited treatment for leprosy. In 1948, he began dispensing Dapsone to leprosy patients living near to the Shirati Mission compound. Word spread like a tropical cyclone that a doctor, known to his patients as Obimbo (big man), had "good medicine."

Within weeks, African men, women and children arrived at Shirati for treatment. Some were on foot, others on bicycle or by boat; many had travelled from their homes hundreds of miles distant, across northwestern Tanganyika and from the southern provinces of Kenya.

Settlements close to the Mission soon became crowded with ailing squatters, and resentment flared. Seeing a blessing turning into a nightmare, Dr. Eshleman moved quickly to find a solution.

His bright idea came in the form of a fifteen-acre "no man's" piece land, three miles distant from the Mission, down a secluded dirt road. Here he made plans to build a leprosarium. Patients living within walking distance of the site would remain at home, and receive treatment as outpatients. For these patients, treatment costs would be nominal, no more than twenty shillings (approximately five dollars) per year. If patients could not pay, they would not be refused.

Patients from distant communities would live on the site. They must agreed to build simple living accommodations for themselves in the "Patients' Village" on Leprosarium grounds, for the duration of treatment – up to two years. Leprosy treatment would therefore come at a great personal cost. Only the patient, his or her spouse and their nursing children were allowed to live on the property. Other children, parents, siblings or extended family must find other accommodation.

Looking back on her predecessor's rules, ones she tried to follow to the letter, Elsie defends them.

> The rules were to keep the size of the Patients' Village under control. If we had not made and had not strictly enforced them, we would have had a population far too high to manage. So as hard as it was for many parents, they needed to make arrangements for their children while they were receiving treatment here. Few patients refused. The opportunity to treat the demon that lived with them was too great.

Construction of the Shirati Leprosarium soon commenced, with leprosy patients providing the free labour. A small two-room dispensary went up first, followed by a two-room ward building. This would house patients too ill to live in the Patients' Village. A small chapel was also built on the plot.

As supervisor of the Leprosarium, Dr. Eshelman would continue to reside at the Shirati main compound, and would travel back and forth between the two centers. An overseer, whose house was constructed on Leprosarium grounds, would be in charge when the doctor was not there. Such was the picture when Elsie arrived, in early February 1954.

Chapter Nineteen
"Noze" Elsie Arrives

Elsie recalls her first impressions of what would be her workplace for the next seventeen years:

> The leper colony[1] was a lovely large plot of land that lay between a wall of high rock and the lake. But it was an overgrown mess. The vegetation grew tall and wild everywhere. It would have to be cleared before anything else was done.

Her gaze then traveled to the buildings themselves. She laughs: "There was room for improvement there too. The dispensary had walls but no roof." Raised on a farm where work was as routine as breathing, Elsie rolled up her sleeves and immediately got cracking on improvements and beautification of the property.

Landscaping would come first. This was work that Elsie could supervise herself, with no cost to the mission. She knew it wouldn't be hard to convince the patients to do the work. "They were so anxious to receive treatment, that they'd do this work gladly."

Elsie's plan was to grow vegetables on the land around the Leprosarium. "It would keep the patients busy and would also feed them." Produce left over would be sold, providing an income for the patients who gardened. Over the next months, brush, logs, stones and rocks were cleared. Then cultivation of the soil, by hand, commenced. Cabbage, squash, peas, beans and corn seeds were then planted.

In his book *Green Grows the Willow*, former Shirati physician Lester Eshelman, describes the spectacular fruits of Elsie's project:

> From the walls of the huts to the lake edge, every square inch of black soil became a lush garden. Corn grew in every

[1] The term "leper" is now politically incorrect. "Persons with leprosy" is the preferred term, focusing on the disease, not the person. At the time the word "leper" was acceptable and this word will be used in the context of the times.

> sliver of soil between the rocks. Papaya trees developed rapidly and in several years each palm-like stem clustered a bushel of fruit. Even with 300 to 400 people crowded on this twenty-acre lakeside area, surplus often went for sale to the community market.

Elsie now moved on to building renovation and expansion. She knew that even though her patients would do this labour too, money for building supplies would be dependent on the Mission's finances. Still slowly and surely, due primarily to Elsie's determination, the Leprosarium grew.

Her first construction project was the long-anticipated Assembly Hall. As the number of her patients increased, the line-ups for medication at the dispensary had grown long. Even for Africans used to the heat of the day, the wait was an exhausting one. An alternative was needed. The hall would serve too as a place of worship.

Open-concept in design, with pillars holding up the roof, the Assembly Hall's glass-less windows allowed the refreshing breeze blowing off Lake Victoria into the hall. The Assembly Hall was only the beginning of Elsie's renewal projects. She became the proverbial "squeaky wheel" pleading her beloved Leprosarium's case with Mission administration. And her persistence paid dividends. Over Elsie's seventeen years at Shirati, the Leprosarium grew into a self-contained village with a number of medical buildings as well as storage facilities, toilets, a school and church.

Furnishing the buildings took even more perseverance. "It was nothing to wait for a couple of years for furniture," Elsie says. "The Leprosarium just seemed to come at the very end of people's priority lists for spending money." Still occasionally, Elsie's ship would come in. In a letter to Mary King at year's end, 1956, she rejoices:

> Well they are finally making a few cupboards for the Leprosarium. We have been waiting almost two years for a few articles of furniture and have been getting along with store boxes – no chairs and no sink.

Once one project was completed Elsie's busy brain conceived of another. And she was in her element.

Chapter Twenty
That Darned Swahili!

Elsie's battle with the Swahili language progressed much slower than her beautification projects. Her progress – or lack of it – is best tracked through her letters to Mary King. A letter on Feb 17, 1954, two weeks after her arrival at Shirati, sees her struggling – and procrastinating. "I am supposed to be studying five hours a day for my first exam in three weeks." May 1954, four months into her placement still sees Elsie in a state of discouragement:

> Even as I learn Swahili, I'm still not communicating well with patients as most don't speak it. I need to rely almost totally on patients who can translate Luo, the dialect most patients speak to Swahili – not English.

Fortunately population growth came to her rescue. As the numbers of new missionaries increased in the Musoma area, it was apparent that language classes where conversation was stressed over book learning would be helpful. Several missionaries who had mastered the language offered these classes and Elsie welcomed them. The classes also helped change her attitude about having to learn a new language.

> At first, I had focused on studying the language so I could pass the exam. And I had detested and avoided that time. Then one day I shifted it in my head and decided I would learn Swahili for myself, not for passing an exam. And that seemed to get me over the hump and I started to really pick the language up.

Elsie's final examination was oral, where she'd be tested on delivering a short scripture lesson in Swahili. She passed this test with flying colours. "I'd been teaching Sunday School classes in Swahili by then and was pretty confident," she recalls. By November 1956, almost two years after her arrival at Shirati, Elsie's battle with Swahili was a thing of the past.

Years later when Elsie had returned to Canada and was nursing at the Kitchener-Waterloo Hospital, she was asked to help with an African patient from Zanzibar who could speak no English. She entered the man's room and said to him in confident Swahili: "Shikamu." This was the usual formal greeting which translates literally to mean "I take hold of your feet."

> The man was shocked and said to me in Swahili, "Mara haba," meaning "how come you are speaking in my language?" We continued to chat for quite a while and then I moved on.
>
> As I passed the other patient's bed, he said to me in German: "nicht verstehe," (I do not understand). That I could figure out too. I thought it was funny that a person like me who found language learning very hard could get by in all three languages.

Elsie's exposure to Swahili today is limited to the annual summer get-together of Shirati alumni. "We all make a point of speaking to each other in Swahili, even if it is a few words." The depth of her immersion in the language sometimes makes itself evident in her sleep. "Every once and a while I'll dream in Swahili," she laughs.

Chapter Twenty-One
Sad, Sad Stories

Just days into her job, Elsie writes to Mary, speaking of the rapidly-growing number of leprosy patients arriving daily to seek treatment:[1]

> We have almost 200 names on our new roll of leper patients. There are more and more coming every day, and we will have to be turning away patients soon. We do not have room for everybody who needs us.

By late February, 1954, the numbers have swelled to 300 patients. One hundred of them are residents of the Patients Village, swelling its numbers to fifty-four huts. June sees seventy-five huts with 150 residents. Residential numbers have grows to 200 by October and by year's end, Elsie's rolls counted 386 patients, with 291 living on the plot. "I see no end in sight to the numbers of patients" she writes to Mary.

Her prediction of imminently needing to turn patients away was soon realized. "It's so very hard to do," she says in a letter. "It's not as though you can say 'go to some other hospital,' because there is no other place they can go." Refusing treatment was harder knowing the fate of many of these people in the "outside world." Within the Luo tribe, the predominant ethnic group in the western Lake Victoria region, lepers were tolerated. For other tribes, treatment was not so kind. In a letter to Mary, Elsie tells a sad story:

> Mrs. L. was telling me that in a tribe around Musomo, if a leper patient is about to die, they tie them with ropes and drag them out of the house. They then take them to a certain type of tree, cut the tree down so that it traps them and then leave the body for the hyenas to devour.

[1] The Shirati Leprosarium was the first of its type in western Tanganyika. Patients came from up to several hundred miles to receive treatment.

Generally chatty and upbeat in her letters home, Elsie's words occasionally paint a somber portrait of the physical ravages of leprosy.

> A bad case arrived at the plot today – the worst I've seen so far. It was a man who had ulcers all over his body and they had oozed right through the clothes that he was wearing. He hadn't taken the clothes off for a long time and the clothes were stuck right to his skin. So we had to soak him in a tub of water to loosen the fabric so we could get the clothes off. Even then skin came off.

Another pitiable case on Elsie's rolls was a woman with a toddler, whose husband deserted her.

> She has large ulcers on her feet and walks with a stick, with difficulty. She is not able to carry the child so the child stumbles a few yards behind crying. We give her food as she needs it and I gave her a blanket the other day. She seems very appreciative.

Having subsisted in the shadows of life for so long, the patients who arrived at Elsie Cressman's Leprosarium were full of gratitude. "I wish you could see the faces of people light up as we finally tell them that we will accept them." With no hope on "the outside," some of the more severe and disfigured leprosy patients remained at the Leprosarium for years on end.

Chapter Twenty-Two
"Be it Ever so Humble..." The Patients' Village

Patients who lived near Shirati could carry on their daily lives, only needing to come to the Leprosarium twice weekly for treatment. For those from farther away, leprosy treatment necessitated significant life changes. There was no other option than to move to Shirati and build temporary shelter on the Leprosarium grounds. In an early letter to Mary, shortly after her arrival, Elsie describes her first impression of these homes.

> They're very small, with only one room, made of sticks and mud, but solid under all but the worst weather conditions. I've heard that once when a cyclone blew through the area there wasn't any damage.

No rent was charged for the use of the land the houses sat on. Materials were found around the Leprosarium plot. Patients fed themselves. In their recollection of Shirati, *Green Grows the Willow*, Dr. Lester and Lois Eshelman recall Dr. Merle Eshelman's advice to his patients: "Eat heartily of fish. This meat will make you strong."[1] Elsie sang the same tune once she stepped into Dr. Merle's shoes. She writes to a friend:

> We've named one of the paths in the Patients' Village "Fish Market Street." It's lined with fish nets hanging to dry from the huts. Walking along you'll likely see some of the patients making nets. There are plenty of fish in the lake which is such a great advantage. Good food is essential in leprosy treatment.

---

[1] Eshleman, J. Lester and Lois, *Green Grows the Willow: Shirati Hospital, 1935-2005 and 1935-2007: The Medical Development of Shirati Hospital with its International Relationships*. (Morgantown, PA: Mastoff Printers, 2007), 62-67.

The Eshelmans also comment on the business success of the patients' fishing enterprises. "There was more than enough fish caught to feed the village. So excess was sold to eager local villagers."

Caring for the Leprosarium gardens was also the responsibility of Elsie's patients. When hippos could be kept out of the plot, the vegetables also filled hungry stomachs. Some patients kept goats or chickens, and a few creative ones wove baskets or built canoes. These they sold or bartered for food.

Patients could also earn a bit pocket money doing extra work around the Shirati grounds. But Elsie discouraged work for cash. "Africans didn't understand money; if you gave it to them, they'd lose it, give it away, or spend it foolishly. I learned to give them only a bit of money at one time."

Chapter Twenty-Three
Elsie's Transportation Woes

Elsie's position at Shirati was unique. Other staff went to work on the compound, no more than a few hundred feet from their homes. Elsie had a three mile trek down a dusty dirt road in front of her before she started her workday. With no car, taxi or bus at her disposal, Elsie set off each morning on foot.

It wasn't long before she was chafing at the time – an hour each day – that she wasted going to and from work. And the road was dusty too. Elsie eventually bought an old bicycle. That speeded up the time but pedaling was still hard work under the mid-day African sun.

Then the rains came. East Africa had two rainy seasons – the first a long and heavy series of torrential downpours from March to May; the second brought lighter rains from November to January. During rainy season Elsie's bike ride became a nightmare.

In their book, Lester and Lois Eshelman describe Elsie's challenges:

> For a third of the year, between the compound and the Leprosarium lay a slough of muck about 100 yards in width. This challenged anyone to attempt a crossing. But Elsie managed to wade and jump stones to report for the daily vigil.[1]

Elsie recalls her own heroic exercises during these challenging adventures:

> Even at the crest of the hill, the road was muddy. And it became muddier still, the closer I rode to the bottom. A creek had formed in the valley and the only way I could get across it was to carry my bike. I was terrified I'd slip on the stones. Having made it most times, I'd get on the

[1] Eshleman, J. Lester and Lois, *Green Grows the Willow, Shirati Hospital, 1935-2005 and 1935-2007: The Medical Development of Shirati Hospital with its International Relationships*. Morgantown, PA: Mastoff Printers, 2007, p. 62-67.

bike and ride up the hill.

She soon gave up wearing her nurses' whites and hose. "I took to wearing a dark-coloured skirt, light blouse and bare legs." No small fashion decision for a conservative Mennonite girl!

Elsie's second year battling the mud saw her contemplating a change. "I've been thinking seriously about the possibilities of living in the overseer's house on the plot." The drawbacks to this move were primarily social. She'd miss the camaraderie with the other Shirati staff. There had to be another option.

She found it in a used motorcycle that had seen better days. But within days of putting the "jalopy" on the road, she regretted her purchase. She laments to Mary in a letter: "The motorcycle worked good for a couple of days then I couldn't start it. I was back to the mud and the bicycle."

Poor Elsie! One can only imagine the worries felt at home by Curtis and Amanda Cressman, on hearing of their daughter's transportation woes. For her second Christmas in Africa they sent to her enough money to buy a new motor scooter. In a January 1956 letter to friends, Elsie barely contains her excitement about arrival of her smart, red, Italian-made Lambretta motor scooter, which she affectionately christens "Bretty":

> Yes, my scooter Bretty came shortly before Christmas and has been put to good use. I now don't see how I ever did without her. I'm still waiting for the license for her, or I would have gone on some longer hikes already.

Not that Bretty made Elsie's trip to the leprosarium any easier in the mud of rainy season. "Given Bretty's weight I couldn't risk her slipping on the descent to the water ... and I sure couldn't carry her across the muddy water." She was back on her trusty bicycle.

Then a miracle happened. Recognizing that Elsie was worth her weight in African gold – and then some – Shirati administration saw that she was transported in the Mission's car during rainy season. The trusty Bretty did yeo-woman service the rest of the year.

Chapter Twenty-Four
Rules, Morals and Ethics

Overwhelmed by the population explosion, both at the Leprosarium and in the Patients' Village, Elsie soon realized she needed to put some hard and fast rules in place. Maintaining order during medication distribution was her primary goal and she announced her rules in the Assembly Hall as patients waited for medication.

- "Patients must be orderly or risk losing their medication."
- "No shoes; no pills."
- "Patients must listen attentively to a Bible message before medication."
- "After medication, patients are required to sit quietly on the assembly hall benches until let out row by row."

Even with these controls, the growing patient numbers began to overwhelm Elsie. But turning desperate, sick people away was even harder for her to deal with. She shared her frustrations through her letters: "More and more patients coming and me trying hard to refuse and doing a poor job of it," she laments. "Each time I think: we will take these few and then this will be the last. But the last never seems to come."

Later she shares more self-criticisms:

> I always thought that a person should give a good answer then stick to it. Well I haven't been carrying it out. New patients come and ask to be taken in and I tell them that I'm sorry we cannot. Then I quickly leave before I soften and feel mean for refusing. The next day the same patient is still on the porch and I practically have to walk over him to get to the dispensary and I tell him no again.

An even more heart-wrenching task was to part youngsters from parents. Rules stated that huts in the Patients' Village must house only the patient, his or her spouse and a nursing child. The rule was not only to keep numbers from growing out of control but to protect children from contracting the disease. Elsie describes such a situation:

> This patient insisted that they had no one to keep their child, but I knew this to be untrue. Finally I set a date and said that if he did not take the child by then I would refuse his leprosy medicine. And I did. Then he came with tears in his eyes saying he would go in the morning with the child.

Still, in reflecting on her almost two decades at the Shirati Leprosarium, Elsie says there were few serious discipline problems. This shouldn't be surprising given her patients' circumstances – individuals so beaten down by the misfortunes of their lives that little, if any, spark of contrariness remained. And given Elsie's role as "Fairy Godmother," keeper and dispenser of the magic pills that took away hurts, it would have been unthinkable for them to cross her. "They loved me, and were respectful, kind and courteous to me," Elsie remembers, smiling.

Yet human nature as it is, incidents needing correcting did occur. And on the rare occasion when someone did step out of line, Elsie's take-charge personality was up for the challenge. In her eyes, "immorality" between men and women was her Leprosarium's #1 sin.

Raised in a conservative Mennonite home, she viewed sexual relations as ones only shared between a man and woman, after the vows of marriage had been taken. Even then, sex should take place primarily for the procreation of children.

But this mind-set was born of Western thinking, as Elsie soon learned. "If an African man wanted a woman in his bed, the woman had no rights to refuse." And if his urge occurred in the dispensary of a Leprosarium? No matter.

When sexual adventures happened under Elsie Cressman's roof – as they did occasionally – and were discovered, then punishment needed to be meted out. A warning to the offender was followed by his banishment if he offended again.

Petty stealing and physical assault between patients also occurred, and Elsie dealt expeditiously with these. A more common, and unpleasant issue was improper use of the latrine. Before modern sanitation was installed at the Leprosarium, not until the 1970's, toilets consisted of a cement pad, a hole in the cement, and a chain. Upgraded models came with a privacy door.

When nature called, the user approached the cubicle and positioned him or herself over the hole. The chain was then pulled, which directed water down a pipe and washed waste into the hole. Uncouth by North American standards, it was a step up the sanitary ladder for many Africans – and a terrifying procedure to boot.

Before coming to the Leprosarium, most patients had performed their toilet in the bush. Evidence was left behind, uncovered, for inspection by the gods. The notion of waste disappearing down a hole was not only mystifying but unnatural to some. For others, the thought of mixing their waste with another's was inviting the gods' revenge. Elsie recalls her task in this respect:

> Some patients would refuse to direct urine and excrement at the hole. They'd deposit it beside the hole. And who was going to get them to do it the right way? Me, of course. It was distasteful, but the teaching needed to be done. And eventually they'd get it right.

Elsie had appointed a number of dependable and trustworthy patients to assist her when discipline was necessary. But when one of her most reliable helpers "went bad," Elsie was beside herself with worry. Over several letters to her pen friend Mary, she relates the sorry saga of Lucas:

> Lucas was one of my most trusted and intelligent helpers. He assisted me doling out the medications and helped me with discipline. Then one day, one of my other fellows told me that Lucas was down at one end of the compound shouting and threatening other patients.

Elsie went to see, and the fellow's report was accurate. Lucas' behaviour became so violent that Elsie called for help at the main compound, and her former right-hand man ended up in one of the hospital's isolation huts until his mood quieted.

The day after the incident, Elsie went to visit him.

> So I walked into the hut where he was being kept and as soon as he saw me, he started to yell. He picked up a bed pan and shouted that he was going to throw it at me. I talked him out of it and warned him that he'd be in trouble if he did.

What Elsie didn't know until a "little bee" whispered in her ear was that Lucas, alone among patients having the keys to the Leprosarium stores, had been pilfering medication on a regular basis for himself. "He thought the more he took, the faster his leprosy would be healed," Elsie explains, "but all it did was make him very agitated."

Eventually Lucas's fit passed and he returned to his position of responsibility. "He promised me he'd never do it again," Elsie reports. "And he didn't."

Chapter Twenty-Five
Death ... and Life

Ruth and Elsie Cressman, born two years apart were close as sisters. Both were caring, compassionate women who had chosen to dedicate their careers to helping others. After high school, Ruth took her nurses training at St. Mary's Hospital, inspiring her kid sister to do the same two years later. Some years later, Ruth chose to upgrade her nursing qualifications and left Canada for Goshen Mennonite College to obtain her BA in Nursing. Ruth then left for the American mid-west where she took midwife's training and joined a practice which had been started by American midwife-pioneer Mary Breckinridge.

It was here the two sisters' personal paths diverged. In Arkansas, Ruth had met Clifford Strubar, a missionary farmer. The two married in 1955 and Ruth became pregnant immediately. Her pregnancy was a difficult one as she battled jaundice and toxemia. Today both conditions are treated with effective medication and, if needed, with hospital care. "But back then, in rural Arkansas with a Mennonite country doctor, she wasn't looked after properly," Elsie says. Letters from Ruth to Elsie in Africa usually carried with them mentions of her pregnancy health struggles. Elsie became concerned for her older sister.

During her second year at Shirati, on her return from a week's holidays, she found several letters waiting for her. One was from her mother, and Elsie eagerly tore open the blue Aerogramme letter form. The news that greeted her caused her heart to skip a beat. Ruth had died in childbirth. The child she bore, a boy had lived only a day when he also passed away.

Elsie looked at the date the letter was written and realized it was more than two weeks old. Both Ruth and her infant had long been buried by now. "I felt terrible, but what was there I could do to help anyone?" she asks, pragmatically. Elsie hid her sorrows in work. This wouldn't be the last time she would choose this diversion.

More than fifty years later, she reflects back with certain regret at the needless death of her beloved sister. "If she had only been hospitalized when the toxemia got bad, she could have been helped. But she chose not to. That was just the way it was."

Fulfilled in her primary role of Nurse-Manager at the Shirati Leprosarium, within weeks of her arrival she'd taken on a second job of Leprosarium midwife. By the time she departed Africa seventeen years later, she had delivered over 2000 African babies.

In rural Africa, babies usually came into the world with only one woman-attendant. Few had any other training for their role, other than having born children themselves. Women of high standing in a village often found themselves in this role. Although most births occurred without medical incident either to the infant or mother, sometimes complications arose – complications that an untrained birth attendant couldn't circumvent. This made delivering women very nervous. "So when they found out that I could deliver babies, they all wanted to choose me," Elsie says. "It was as if an angel had dropped down to help them!"

She soon learned that the "western" style of giving birth was not the African way. Women usually bore their infants while squatting in an upright position. So "when in Rome do as the Romans do" became Elsie's attitude too and she acquiesced to their wishes. For those who preferred to lie, she had a carpenter build a slanted delivery bed at the Leprosarium's maternity ward. This facilitated the passage of bodily fluids during the birth.

Babies had the habit of being born at night and Elsie recalls frequently being wakened in her own bed by a tap on her bedroom window. It was the Leprosarium overseer's reporting that: "the baby is coming." On these occasions, she had the use of the hospital car to drive to her patient. Usually Elsie arrived in time to deliver the baby. On one occasion, she was delayed and the results were tragic.

> One of the older women was acting as midwife until I arrived. She met me at the door telling me that she'd delivered triplets. But when I got to the room, I could only see two babies in bed with the mother. "Where is the third", I asked her. She looked evasive and said she didn't know.
>
> I was pretty sure I knew the story. I found the third infant dead under the bed. It was bad luck in some African societies to deliver three babies, and she had smothered it.

Elsie found African birthing rituals fascinating, if incomprehensible. One dictated that infants must remain in the family dwelling for 4 days after the delivery. To bring an infant out into the world before this was inviting danger and illness. Another stated that a nursing mother couldn't take charge of another baby during this time or the entire family would be cursed.

A potentially dangerous superstition involved infants and home-brewed banana beer. After birth the newborn was given beer to cause them to vomit it. African mothers could now rest, assured that the "dirt" inside their infant was now washed out of its body.

Superstitions aside, Elsie had generally positive feelings about the African mothers whose paths she crossed. "Most African women I knew were naturally very good mothers," Elsie says.

Still infant cleanliness practices took some getting used to. In a letter to Mary King, Elsie passes on the African style of dealing with dirty noses and dirty bottoms:

> Few African babies wear diapers and most are naked. Those diapers that are used are more rag than anything

> and only keep the solid in – certainly not the urine. When mothers think their baby going to have a BM they hold it up off the ground and let it fall. Then they cover it up with leaves.

And with no handy Kleenex box to deal with runny noses, African women used what nature gave them to deal with the mess. "They'd wipe their babies' faces and runny noses with back of hand and then wipe it on grass. When the mess was too widespread to clean with a hand, women had no hesitation about licking their children to keep them clean."

Given the affection that Africans felt for their children, their disregard for leprosy transmission was horrifying to her. She'd learned that the leprae bacillus couldn't be passed on from mother to unborn child. But it could, and would be transmitted in skin to skin contact, such as infants lying with mothers to sleep and bare-bodied babies being carried on mothers' backs. Her frustration is best expressed in letters home:

> We are trying to keep untainted children from living on the leper plot and our concerns seem to fall on deaf ears. Most Africans don't care if their children get leprosy for they just don't think ahead. They hope they won't get it but they don't understand the disease.

Africans' lack of understanding of western medication also caused Elsie sleepless nights. A feverish infant was brought to her for treatment. Suspecting malaria, Elsie gave the babe an injection of the drug Chloroquine.

> As soon as I gave the baby the injection it went into convulsions. I immediately ran warm water in a basin and placed the baby in, hoping that water would relax the baby enough that the convulsions would stop. But it didn't and its heart stopped. The baby died.

Only after the tragedy did Elsie learn that when her baby became ill the woman had given it a dose of her own medication. The drug sent the wee one's system into toxic shock.

> From then on I wouldn't allow my patients to leave the clinic with medication in hand – especially if they had young children. I had learned not to trust their judgment when it came to medications. They'd make them sick or kill then – not from malice, but from ignorance.

Elsie estimates that she delivered on average one to two babies every week. She took from these experiences knowledge that she would use when her career turned to midwifery.

CHAPTER TWENTY-SIX
Serengeti Adventure

Time away from work took two forms at Shirati: holidays which were of a one-month duration and came every year and furloughs which lasted twelve months, and occurred usually after five years of service. Elsie used the one-month holidays for travel in Africa.

An inveterate letter-writer, Elsie's chatty epistles paint vivid pictures of the African safari in mid-century. Her letters also give insight into the spirit of a veritable adventuress, a woman for whom no challenge was insurmountable or challenging.

First on Elsie's list to visit was Serengeti National Park, within driving distance of Shirati. The sprawling nature preserve had been open only for two years when Elsie visited in 1954. Serengeti was pure "roughing it in the (African) bush!"

> A gang of four dress-clad, Oxford shoe-wearing Mennonite missionary nurses, including Elsie set out for the six-hour drive to Serengeti. Elsie was at the wheel of a gas-guzzling, oil belching VW camper. "I was game for most anything anyway," she laughs.

An hour into the trip Elsie met her first obstacle. At the crest of a hill, she spied a fast-rushing stream at the bottom, the result no doubt of recent heavy rains. Pausing momentarily, Elsie gunned the engine and pelted down the grade, planning to make made a run at the water. "You had to keep going at a good speed to make it up the other side," she chuckles.

With her passengers, no doubt, holding on for dear life, the jalopy made the mad dash and emerged still chugging, on the other side of the stream. Problem one dealt satisfactorily!

But now the VW was belching black smoke. No problem. Every so often Elsie would give it a shot of engine oil, and carry on her way. In this fashion, the girls arrived at N'Dabaka, the front gates of Serengeti National Park. Surprisingly they seemed to be the only visitors seeking admission.

> The guard told us that nobody had been through for the last three days. The roads were pretty well un-navigable due to the mud inside the Park. But he had only to take a good look at our van to see that we'd probably seen worse on the way there. He suggested we come back another time, but we decided that nothing could match what we'd traveled through already.

With stern words of caution, the guard opened Serengeti's gates to the visitors, warning the women too that there would be no guide anywhere close if they got into trouble. Most of them had gone home until the weather improved. Within minutes, Elsie and her friends knew that the guard's cautions about un-navigable roads had not been hyperbole.

> I decided that I'd fare better if I could navigate to the left or right of the holes, driving on an angle with the wheels up the left or right side of the shoulders. The only fly in that ointment was that the shoulders were steep – very steep. Before I knew it, the car was on such a tilt that everybody had to lean the opposite way or else we'd tip right over. That strategy seemed to work until the tires began to spin and we were mired – still leaning badly. So I ordered everybody out to push – Oxfords and dresses no excuse!

And push they did. The van began to move and Elsie soon righted it. Ahead, the path looked less perilous and the girls were on their way.

A steady procession of wildlife wandered free across the Serengeti Plains, some at close range. The sight helped the nurses forget what they'd been through since they left Shirati.

> We saw hundreds of zebras, gazelle and wildebeest. In the distance there was the odd giraffe, and we glimpsed a few cheetahs lying under the trees. It was wonderful, as none of us had ever seen animals like this before, except in books.

Visitors who planned to stay overnight at the park could reserve a sleeping tent complete with cots. Guests could also partake of some basic grub in the Serengeti dining tent. As the light waned, Elsie's party was eager for a meal and after that a soft pillow for the night. It was almost dark when the belching VW pulled into the residential area of the park. The weary nurses climbed out to head to the camp mess for their supper. With few other visitors in the park, the Shirati gang had their choice of table, and line-ups for the cafeteria-style meal were non-existent.

Just as they were beginning dinner, a bellow was heard outside. All conversation abruptly halted within. "It didn't take a lot of imagination to know it was some big cat on the loose pretty close," Elsie recalls, "and boy, did it send a shiver up and down one's spine." An announcement was made to the few assembled diners that indeed several of their big cats were up to monkey business. Guests were advised to remain safe within the dining tent. "No one needed much convincing, given the racket that was going on outside," Elsie chuckles.

When the pride had relocated, guests headed to their sleeping tents. "We were assured that staff was keeping a watch on them all night," Elsie says, "but you could still hear them roaring and not too far away. So nobody was perfectly relaxed." Despite the night's adventures, everyone in the party had a restful sleep.

Day Two of the Great Serengeti Adventure dawned, with roads no better than the day before. The spectacular scenery took the nurses' minds off the bumpy ride. As they left the Park, the guard recognized them and laughed.

> Apparently after we drove off the first day, he'd bet the other attendant that a woman driving a beat-up van through such mud would never have made it there and back again. But I'd proved him wrong. When I asked him how the roads were outside the park, he said if I could drive through Serengeti at the end of the rainy season I could handle anything out there.

Elsie downplays the part she played in getting her passengers there and home again.

> I was always up for any adventure, so bad roads, an old belching van and mouthy lions were nothing to me. There really wasn't much I wouldn't take on. But was I fearless? No. I just was careful and tried to use my head!

And a pretty level head it was. Elsie returned to Serengeti several times over her twenty-three years in Africa. No subsequent visit had the same fond memories as her first.

Chapter Twenty-Seven
Mount Kilimanjaro

"Everyone climbed Mount Kilimanjaro at least once while they were in Africa," Elsie says. Never one to hang back in savouring adventure, Elsie added trekking up the fabled mountain to her book of life's experiences. The trip was planned for Elsie's one-month furlough in December 1955. She'd make the five-day climb with her Shirati colleagues Alta Weaver, Miriam Buckwalter and Don Jacobs. It was the 40-year- old Alta's second try at completing the climb. Nausea and weakness had stopped her a year before.

Called "the world's highest walkable mountain" Kilimanjaro at 19,321 feet is the highest peak on the African continent.[1] Once an active volcano, Kilimanjaro has two peaks, Kibo and Mawenzi. Unlike more formidable mountains such as Mount Everest, Kilimanjaro is considered an accessible climb, attracting both experienced and novice climbers. Starting in tropical climate, the climb soon grows chilly, then cold as climbers ascend through five climate zones, ending in ten degrees Fahrenheit. As the air cools, it grows thin, making breathing and movement difficult.

The ascent is broken into three day-long climbs; the descent takes a speedy two days. Food for the journey, guides and overnight accommodation are arranged through one of the hotels at the base of the mountain. Climbers bunk for the succeeding nights in bare essentials huts and are up at the crack of dawn for the long day's trek.

Primed and eager for the adventure before them, the Shirati party met with their guides and prepared for the ascent. Alta Weaver, having failed in her previous attempt had made plans to ensure her expedition

[1] "Mount Kilimanjaro National Park." www.tanzaniaparks.com.

would be a success this time out. In her book *Journey Through Time*, she shares her thoughts:

> If at first you don't succeed, try, try again ... this time I had a guide just for myself. I told him under no circumstances should he allow me to turn about before I reached the top ... I was also in better physical shape.[2]

It wasn't long before Elsie began to wonder at her own chances for success. She'd begun the climb in a cotton dress but had packed long pants and jacket for the colder days ahead. She'd made a strategic error though in choice of footwear. "I was wearing my nurses Oxfords," she chuckles, "a big mistake. I should have had hiking shoes."

Despite the disadvantage, Elsie Cressman was no quitter, nor was she delicate. "There was no way I would have stopped, hurting feet or not." Still the prospect of a 33-mile ascent in pedestrian shoes must have been daunting. The first day's climb afforded spectacular scenery upwards through the rainforest, with hikers having an eagle's eye view of the surrounding countryside. After a stop for lunch, the trek continued, up, up, up. The vegetation thinned and the path became a muddy rut. At quitting time, 5:00 PM, the exhausted group reached Bismarck Hut, their resting place for the night. Elsie calls up her memories:

> This was no first, second or even third class hotel, just rough bunks with dried grass for mattresses. No heating provided but everybody got a hot-water bottle. And we needed it. Good luck to those of us needing to use the facilities in the night. It was an outdoor privy with no door!

Into Day Two of the trek, Elsie's group had left the rainforest behind and climbed into a dense cloud cover. "It was a funny sensation and made you feel pretty cut off from the world," she recalls. Clear cold streams ran along the trail and the hikers were glad to stop for a refreshing drink. By afternoon, it had become tough slogging due to

---

[2] Weaver, Alta. *Journey through Time, Passed Between Hearts in Family, Home and Africa*. (Ephrata, Pa: Grace Press, Inc. 2008) 297.

the high altitude. "You could feel it in your chest and it became really tough to keep one foot moving ahead of the other." Elsie changed into her trousers and donned her coat for the afternoon's climb. The exhausted group fell into bed at the second overnight rest stop, Peter's Hut. Sleep came almost immediately for the weary hikers.

The morning of the Third Day started optimistically with one of the twin peaks, Mawenzi, coming clearly in view. At noon, with ten miles to go to the third hut, Kibo, the adventurers approached the saddle between Mawenzi and Kibo and stopped for nourishment. They need it. At 14,000 feet altitude, the air was reed-thin, making breathing laborious. Bouts of nausea persisted. At this altitude, skin chapped and became raw. Guides advised hikers to smear a thick layer of Vaseline on any exposed skin. At 6:00 PM they reached Kibo Hut, their third night's accommodation. A surprise awaited them in the cabin. Elsie recalls:

> Two guys who had thought they'd be able to camp outdoors for the night had had second thoughts and asked if they could bunk down on the floor of the cabin for the night. It made things pretty crowded but how could you turn them away?

After a hurried supper, the group turned in for an early start on the last day's ascent. The wake-up call would be 1:00 AM. Much experience with unseasoned trekkers had shown the guides that up to 15 hours of hiking would be needed on this final day to reach the summit. There was unscheduled excitement ahead of that goal!

> We were awoken with a crash. Our "houseguests" had decided to sleep under the table to be out of the way and I guess one of them had to get up in the night to use the toilet and forgot he was where he was. His head hit the table, he let out a roar, the table tipped over and everything on it went clattering across the room. Well you can imagine how easy it was to settle back to sleep after that!

The 1:00 AM call came agonizingly early, but for Elsie the trek was well worth the lack of sleep. "The early going, under the stars and moon of a Tanganyikan night was exhilarating." This mood quickly gave way to exhaustion.

> By now we were encountering snow and the air was very cold. But that wasn't the difficulty; the problem was pushing one foot ahead of the other. The air was so thin that you felt absolutely lifeless. You just felt like you wanted to fall down and sleep. I'd take one step and rest, then push myself to take another step, and rest. I was making very little progress.

Feeling she was about to falter, Elsie took a guide's arm for support on numerous occasions. Even then, she'd drop back and fall to the ground. "I just wanted them to leave me behind so I could sleep." But press on she did, as did the determined Alta Weaver. Alta records her progress. "This time, my rest stops found me lying on my face. My guide would pull my arm. "Get going." I leaned on his arm for a good part of the last stretch, with him literally dragging me.[1]

Unfortunately complete victory over Mount Kilimanjaro was not to be realized for the Shirati group. Deep snow halted them somewhat short of the summit. After a rest period, the descent began and the group reached Peter's Hut around 5:00 PM. The day which had begun under the stars ended with a welcome supper and a satisfied, undisturbed, deep sleep. An easy final leg to the Marangu Hotel completed the adventure of a lifetime the next day.

---

[1] Weaver, p. 298.

Chapter Twenty-Eight
More African Travel

Elsie planned no more major holidays over the next several years until her long furlough in 1959. Still she ventured to various African tourist attractions during her shorter vacation periods. Holidays to the seashore were a draw for the sun-loving Elsie, with the seaside resort of Dar-es-Salaam, on the Indian Ocean coast of Tanganyika a favourite.

The vision of a prim Mennonite nurse in modest dress is dispelled by Elsie's self-portrait painted in a letter to Mary King:

> Right now I'm on a beach chair beside the Indian Ocean, with waves breaking in front of me. I'm wearing my bathing suit under one of those cotton seer sucker dresses you gave me. All ready to go for a swim after my dinner settles. The ocean is really wicked at high tide with waves that can roll a person over. I'm afraid to go in alone, so will wait till the others go in.

An inveterate shopper for curios, Elsie had great opportunities to look for treasures in various African big-city markets such as the famous Mombasa market. She was always first in line too when visits to wildlife habitats were an option. Elsie marveled at the coral reef she viewed from the vantage point of an African hollowed-out log. "We found all sorts of colours of star fish, jellyfish, snakes, eels, and a few nice shells." Before conservation made tourist coral reef-scavenging verboten, Elsie snared some attractive coral for a keepsake.

Work and the opportunity to see such marvelous sights took her mind off the second piece of bad news from home she received in the space of two years.

Over the years since her diagnosis as a diabetic, Amanda Cressman's health had been precarious. Raised Amish, she followed the ways of her people and sought naturopathy or other alternative therapies for her condition, rather than the recommended insulin. "Mother was always experimenting with this and that," Elsie recalls. "Usually they did little good and her condition got worse as she aged."

One day after attending a social event in the community, Amanda returned home, not feeling well. She took to her bed, and before long, her breathing became laboured. Curtis decided she needed hospital care and he tool her by car to St. Mary's Hospital in Kitchener. Medical staff saw Amanda's condition as serious. but assured Curtis that his wife would be "OK." After getting her settled, he returned home to do evening chores.

The phone rang just as Curtis entered the house. It was the hospital. Amanda had gone into diabetic shock shortly after he left. Within minutes her heart stopped and she was pronounced dead on August 10, 1956. Amanda Cressman was only 63 years of age.

As had been the case with the death of Ruth, Elsie learned of her mother's death by letter. There was no way to reach her by phone and it appears that even sending a telegram was not an option for Curtis Cressman. "Father had considered sending a telegram but decided against it because he thought I was on another holiday," Elsie offers.

As had been the case after Ruth's death, Elsie's pragmatism won out over emotions. "What could I have done? I certainly didn't have the money to fly home and it would've taken me so long to come by boat." Elsie buried herself in work as she had done during other low points in her life. In a letter to Mary she opens the door to her heart just a little.

> I never really expected it (Amanda's death) but knew it could happen. I think I always had in mind going home and seeing Mom. It will seem so empty to go home with Ruth and Mom gone and I miss their letters so much. We know God makes no mistakes and has things timed right.

Chapter Twenty-Nine
Long Furloughs

The years slipped by quickly with Elsie firmly in charge of her beloved Leprosarium. More buildings, more staff to assist her, and stability in patient numbers made her job easier too. Elsie took three year-long furloughs between 1959, (an extended one, as she had to undergo back surgery at home) and 1970, her last.

As she earned no salary during this time, it was necessary for her to work. With Elsie's nursing credentials, this was never a problem. One short-term nursing job was at a tuberculosis hospital in Toronto. She broadened her expertise too by taking additional nursing courses. Filling in any extra time, Elsie also did considerable public speaking at church and social groups across the province.

Invariably the subject of her perils getting to and from the Leprosarium from her house at Shirati came up. Not one to whine or complain, Elsie still never failed to arouse sympathy in the listening crowd. After hearing her tale of "Falling off My Bicycle on the Road to the Leprosarium" one group decided to do something to help her situation.

The Youth Group at her home church Biehn Mennonite Church in New Hamburg hatched an ambitious project to raise funds to build Elsie a house at the Leprosarium. Even if she only used it "in a pinch" when a night baby delivery was imminent or when the road was too muddy to traverse, it would make Elsie's life easier, they thought.

And so the "Corn Project" was born. Each member of the Youth Group would plant, tend and harvest sweet corn from their home gardens. The corn would then be sold at roadside stands or other places where city folk flocked to get a taste of the mouthwatering late summer treat. At the end of the summer the Youth Group had raised approximately $1,500 to buy materials to build Elsie's house.

Humbled by the group's kind thoughts and generosity, Elsie

still knew that it was doubtful that she would live in the house permanently.

> The Shirati administration didn't like the idea of me living at the Leprosarium one bit. They felt it was too isolated and I could be the target for break-ins or other problems.

Still the project commenced. A location close to the shore of Lake Victoria had been chosen for its scenic view and the cooling breeze that blew in from the water. The ever dependable 1W boys, Hershey and Cris supervised a local construction company who did the work.

Fabricated of burnt brick, like most other homes in East Africa, Elsie's house would have a kitchen, two bedrooms and shaded front porch. For convenience it would have running water, indoor toilet facilities, but no electricity.

Elsie believes that she stayed in the house a mere handful of times. "And when I did, a night watchman slept on the front porch." It did prove to be a handy guest house for visitors to Shirati. Parties and barbeques were held there too.

Sadly, Elsie's little house eventually fell victim to the whims of nature. Torrential rains in 1962 caused Lake Victoria to rise an unprecedented six feet, and many buildings close to the lake were damaged. Some washed away. Elsie's little house was flooded. Curiously, water levels remained high and structures had to be permanently abandoned.

"And eventually my house was demolished," Elsie recalls. Begun by the enthusiasm of youth people as a way to help a friend, the "Corn Project" ended in disappointment.

Near the end of Elsie's tenure at Shirati she moved into a house on the compound that had been vacated by one of the Mission's overseers. "So I finally got my own house and this one didn't wash away," she laughs.

Chapter Thirty
Jerosa

One day in the spring of 1958, Elsie paid a visit to Shirati's African lab technician, Enoka and his wife Trefina in the couple's home. Trefina had recently had a baby and Elsie was looking forward to seeing how much the little one had grown.

On her arrival, Elsie was surprised to see two babies. One, in the arms of Trefina was the picture of health, happy and robust; the other, being held by Trefina's oldest daughter was "skin and bones." She soon found out the story behind the picture.

Enoka's father, an elderly man had married a young girl who suffered from epilepsy. Sometime after the girl had given birth to a daughter, she died. As it was considered bad luck for a second infant to be cared for by an already-nursing mother (in this case Trefina), the family was searching for a substitute.

> In cases like this, the care of a motherless infant would usually be transferred over to a widow with a cow. But cow's milk was a poor substitute for mother's milk and most likely the infant would die of malnutrition.

The story tugged at Elsie's nurturing heartstrings.

> I couldn't let this happen to such a sweet little baby. I offered to take over her care, at least until her health improved. This was on the understanding that she would be returned to Enoka's family once she was strong and was starting to eat solid food.

The offer was gladly taken up. Elsie says: "Trefina said that God had sent me to take the curse off them."

Elsie needed a bit of time to prepare herself for a baby. There was a small guestroom beside her quarters. There Jerosa (the name Elsie had given her) could sleep. A crib, infant swing and high chair could likely be commandeered somewhere too. She also scrounged a large basin which she could sit in the bathroom sink to give Jerosa her baths. Diapers were fashioned from scraps of cloth found here and there; from one of her own silk panties Elsie fashioned a silk dress for her little ward. "She was so tiny, and I wasn't, so that I had plenty of material," Elsie jokes.

Elsie's initial sense of confidence and excitement about her mission faltered when Trefina brought little Jerosa to Shirati several days later.

> I'll always carry with me the memory of Trefina laying this thin, sickly baby on my bed. I looked down at her and said silently to myself: "This baby is in terrible shape and is surely going to die." I wasn't at all sure I could make her healthy.

Still, not one to back down from a difficult situation, Elsie said goodbye to Trefina and got to work. At six months of age, Jerosa was severely malnourished, weighing only eight pounds.

> I planned to feed her by cup and spoon. This was cleaner than using a bottle and nipple. I would also feed her ugali, with an egg mixed in for richness. I wasn't sure it would work, but it would certainly give her a chance.

Malnutrition wasn't Jerosa's only health concern. She had a fever, a sure sign of malaria, and had ulcers over her head and back. Elsie also wondered if the little girl had tuberculosis. For these conditions Jerosa was treated with Chloroquine and the antibiotic Penicillin. The results were startling. Jerosa started to thrive. Four weeks after her arrival, her weight had jumped by three pounds.

While sure of her own motives, Elsie's decision to nurse an African infant to health was a controversial one on the Shirati compound. Another nurse had done this previously, and while the short-term results were good, the long term ones were less positive. Elsie recalls:

> This nurse took sick babies in to save them, but then she wouldn't give them back to the natural family when

> they became well. This eventually brought on all sorts of problems with the child never fitting in either culture – African or white. One of the Africans that she adopted eventually committed suicide.

When Elsie had made her intentions known at Shirati, she was warned by at least one staff member that she was "playing with fire."

> One of the doctors reminded me of what had happened before. This made me think deeply about the potential risks involved. But, it still boiled down to: "do you try to save the life of a baby or do you let nature take its course?"

She made the doctor a solemn promise that she would return Jerosa to her people before she left on furlough, several months distant. "Knowing I was going on furlough made it easier to set a time that would return her," she says.

Elsie's daily routine changed very little during this time. Leaving the housekeeper in charge of Jerosa while she was at work, she left for the Leprosarium at her usual time, and returned after lunch. Afternoon rest time for Elsie now included Jerosa too. After both were refreshed, it was play, talk and food time.

Elsie spoke to her little African "daughter" in English, not Swahili. "Her native tongue was Luo so learning Swahili would have been no advantage to her." By July, Elsie is reporting to Mary King that Jerosa is a "happy baby, jabbering a lot – not backward in any way." By ten months, "she is creeping; she has seven teeth and is a bright little girl," Elsie brags to Mary.

By now, the staff was taking their meals at the communal Shirati mess, and Elsie took Jerosa each time. She also accompanied Elsie to Sunday church services. Now growing like a weed, Jerosa needed new clothes regularly. Elsie made them out of cotton feedbags. And like any parent she is proud of "her" baby. "She's as good as gold and is just the best little thing."

As Elsie's furlough of 1959 approached, she was torn. Her heart wanted to be Jerosa's mother; her head reminded her that the growing girl needed to return to her people.

> I knew full well that babies taken from their culture have great difficulty fitting in when they get older. I also knew that the Mission Board wouldn't look favourably on me returning home with an African baby in tow. But then on the other hand, I also imagined how much fun it would be to bring her to Canada.

At one point, Elsie contemplates formally adopting Jerosa, but then decides against it. Only weeks before she is to leave for home, she writes to Mary King:

> Jerosa's days with me are numbered. And she'll go back to where I found her in a few weeks. It's good to make the change soon, as she is beginning to talk. It won't get any easier as the days go on.

In preparation for Jerosa's move, the pragmatic Elsie asks Enoka and Trefina's eldest daughter Miriam to come every day for several hours to play and talk to Jerosa. "It would lessen the shock of her leaving me and get her used to her own people." When Jerosa returned to her family, she was a healthy and happy seven-month old.

For the remainder of Elsie's Shirati tenure, she remained close to Enoka's family and watched Jerosa grow up as a "normal" African village girl. Still, she worried that Jerosa didn't receive the same amount of attention and consideration as Enoka and Trefina's other children. Her worries were born out when she realized that Jerosa was not going to school.

> I asked Enoka why this was so. He seemed sheepish and said something that didn't make sense about school already starting and it was too late to send her. This bothered me and I told him that I would pay for her schooling – which I did.

As years passed, it became difficult to maintain her closeness to Jerosa. "She spoke only Luo and I spoke English and Swahili so we couldn't say much to each other."

And sadly, Jerosa's story played out as it did for many young African girls. "She married young, just into her teens and to a drunkard," Elsie states. And as she matured, her early health problems came to the fore. Jerosa's early malnutrition had led to soft pelvic bones. This complicated both of her pregnancies.

Nearing the end of her African sojourn, Elsie went to see Jerosa and her infant. "Her baby looked just as bad as she had when I got her," Elsie says, "and the baby eventually died."

Elsie looks back on her time with baby Jerosa with fondness. "It was great fun, but I never did it again."

Chapter Thirty-One
A Change is Coming

When Elsie first set her foot on African soil in early 1954, the push for independence within the various European colonies on that continent was beginning to bloom. Events over the next decade would bring fruit to this early budding.

Tanganyika had been a British colony since 1919, ceded to that nation by Germany after World War I. It was prized for its coffee, tea, spices and tobacco crops.

Throughout the 1950's, senior government administration in the capital of Dar-es-Salaam was still held by British representatives. The country declared independence in 1961 when it was renamed Tanzania. To make the evolution even more admirable, the transition had occurred without bloodshed. Reformation of social institutions, including the African Christian missions such as Shirati Medical Mission took longer. Since its founding in the mid-1930's, Shirati had been administered by representatives of the American Mennonite Church. It remained firmly in their hands when Elsie arrived in the mid-1950's. By the late 1950's Africans wanted to take their rightful place at the top. Elsie reflects on the evolution:

> We worried if there would be problems and confrontations, but that didn't happen. American doctors and nurses who left on furlough received notice at home that they wouldn't be required to return. By 1970 when I prepared to take my third furlough, there were only two or three American staff left ... and me.

Well off the "beaten path" of reformation at her Leprosarium, even Elsie Cressman eventually began to feel the winds of change.

> I first knew definitely that the change was coming when one day a group of local men showed up at the clinic.

> They said they wanted to talk to the patients. I had no authority to say no, so I took a back seat as they called them together and talked to them.

What Elsie heard left her unsettled, to say the least.

> The speakers said things to turn the patients against me. And from that point on, it was different. There wasn't anything tangible, but it just wasn't the same. I'd been idolized before because of what I'd done for the leprosy patients. Now I was a white woman in control, an authority figure.

Elsie rationalized that she might be spared from the sweeping Africanization of Shirati Medical Mission. "I thought that because of the nature of my work, working with patients that many people wouldn't go near, that I might be kept on." This wish was not granted. A feeling of unease came over her on the day she turned the keys of the Leprosarium dispensary to one of her African overseers. Elsie knew the man was a thief and should not be trusted. She also knew the situation was out of her control. Canadian Mennonite Nurse Elsie Cressman was now an anachronism.

As she prepared to return to North America for her furlough of 1970-71, she mentally prepared for the possibility that she would not return to the Leprosarium.

> I knew there was a chance I wouldn't be going back to Shirati, so I began to think of other alternatives. Working with the natives in the Canadian North was one option that interested me. Another was taking midwife training in England.

Still she held out faint hope that she would return in a year to Africa. Just to reinforce that fond wish, she left some of her belongings behind.

One of Elsie's first stops after returning to North America was to the Eastern Mennonite Mission Board Office in Pennsylvania. She wanted to discuss her options with the Board. What met her when she arrived was a letter sent to the Board from the African Bishop under whose jurisdiction Shirati now fell. “It told me that I wasn’t invited back,” Elsie says. “I wasn’t surprised or deeply upset. By this time I’d worked out a plan that I hoped would be acceptable to the Board – and it wouldn’t cost them anything.”

She’d decided to become midwife.

Chapter Thirty-Two
Elsie in London

Elsie recalls the "pitch" that she fielded to the Mission Board regarding them sending her for midwife training. She'd done some homework ahead of time.

> It wouldn't cost the mission board anything for my tuition at the Salvation Army Maternity Hospital in London, England. There midwives-in-training worked in the hospital as nurses at the same time. So I felt that this would be an ideal position for me to take – good for me and good for the Mission Board.

They agreed and after a period at home and visiting friends, she left for London England. At age 50, Elsie Cressman was reinventing herself.

She joined a class of nine other midwifery students, all Registered Nurses, like herself. They came from various countries around the world. Elsie's long experience delivering babies was unique among her class. "But it mattered not a whit," she offers, a note of bitterness creeping into her voice.

> There was no honour in that, at this hospital. The Sisters (midwifery teachers) never gave me credit for it. I was just a pupil, not a midwife-in-training and I was certainly not a Registered Nurse. I was treated like a pupil and they never let me forget it. We all had to really watch our p's and q's.

Practical experiences were interspersed with book learning. As usual, Elsie thrived on the practical; the studying didn't come as easily. "I had never been a really good book learner and didn't have a good memory,'" she admits, honestly.

Living accommodations in London were in a dormitory-like

setting, on hospital grounds. Most students took their meals in the cafeteria but Elsie chose to cook for herself. She bought a hotplate and some cooking pots at a second-hand store and "saved lots of money that way." Frugal, rural Mennonite ways die hard, even in cosmopolitan London, England.

Elsie had also brought a bicycle with her from Canada and planned to use her free time discovering London. She usually set off solo, preferring to see the city on her own terms.

Safety was never an issue in her mind. "I'd faced naked Luo warriors brandishing spears and crazed Africans threatening me with plates of food," she laughs. "There was nothing I was going to find in London to match that!" Threading her way through London traffic snarls and around double-decker buses intimidated Elsie not in the slightest.

Pupils went on vacation for two weeks, part way through the year. Elsie and a friend decided to see a bit of northern England and Scotland from the window of a coach and booked their seats. Her strongest, but not fondest memories are of English food and English weather.

> I'd had British cooking in colonial Africa but it was British with a taste of African thrown in. And it was good. But this was real British, what I'd call badly-cooked and badly-served. I recall breakfasts most; the English seemed to be fond of stewed tomatoes and the toast was always cold. Yuck!

The final three months of midwives' training was to take place in the field. Supervised by one of the teaching sisters, all trainees would take the role of Primary Midwife for women in the community who were giving birth at home. These "On District" calls were great learning experiences for Elsie and the other trainees. With much laughter, Elsie recalls some of these "flying trips" to various parts of the district.

> I had a bedpan strapped to the back of the bicycle and various delivery instruments shoved into a bag that I carried around my neck. Then I'd careen full-tilt around a corner and the bedpan would come flying off and bounce,

> crashing and banging down a street. Everybody stopping and staring to see what all the commotion was ... Oh yeah, this was great fun.

Alas, the fun ended for Elsie with final exams. She was confident she'd "ace" the practical component and was "fairly confident" she could scrape her way through the written exam. Her prime concern was for the oral. "I'd never felt that expressing myself orally was one of my greater strengths."

In order to be certified to practice in England, pupils would need to pass all three components. Anyone failing any one of the three parts had three months to retry the exam. Results would come by letter.

The student-midwife grapevine held that students receiving a "skinny letter" could expect a positive result from their exam. "Those with a fat envelope, containing the results, plus all the paperwork needed to retry the exam, should expect bad news," Elsie recollects.

Elsie left her oral exam fully expected that her fate would be told in a fat envelope.

> I was nervous and had started the oral off on a bad foot and I never got on track. So I wasn't surprised when the fat letter arrived in the post. Inside it told me what I already knew. I had failed the oral, so in the eyes of the British College of Midwives, I was not a midwife.

Students who had failed any portion of the certification exam had the opportunity to retry it as many times as was necessary. Elsie had no intention of wasting her time in this effort.

> In fact, I couldn't have cared less. I'd come to school for the experience, not the diploma and I'd gotten that. And besides that, England was not where I planned to practice; Canada was, and I had no doubt I could do that.

In a letter to friends, she is clearer in her direction. She says:

> I am thinking in terms of work with the Canadian government in the remote areas of Northern Canada. But I am still open to think of work in East Africa too, if the

Lord leads me that way.

Characteristically she leaves her path up to her Maker. After all, Elsie reasoned, and rightly so, He hadn't steered her wrong up until now.

Part Four

Transition

Chapter Thirty-Three
Somalia

Elsie's next step became clear with a surprise letter she received while she was still in London. It was from the Eastern Mennonite Mission Board and offered her a position at a hospital in Somalia. If she accepted she'd be supervising two other nurses working there. Elsie shares more details: "There'd been a doctor supervising them but he'd left on furlough and decided not to come back. So they were in a crunch. I'd be in charge until another American doctor arrived to take over, in about three months."

Between jobs previously, Elsie wasted little time in responding positively. Africa was where she had made her mark in patient care; Africa was where she felt welcome and comfortable. The letter only reinforced Elsie's belief that her way in life was divinely-directed.

After tying up loose ends in London, in June, 1971, Elsie boarded a flight for (now) Tanzania. She needed to retrieve the belongings she'd left at Shirati when she'd left for her furlough over a year before. Elsie was curious to see the changes that she'd heard were happening at her old Leprosarium. Her letter written a few days after her arrival at Shirati records these impressions.

> I was showered with gifts of food and had lots of invitations out to eat good African ugali and chicken. The Leprosarium has had a bit of throwing around of staff and has suffered. My old overseer Musalinga feels he can't work and must resign. I feel satisfied now that my work at Shirati is finished and others must carry on. I am glad for the years that I had there and grateful that I could see a modern leprosy clinic established before I had to leave.

While Elsie was surely happy in her knowledge that the modern Leprosarium was up and running, one detects a hint of regret in her words. Surely it would have been running better if it had been her at the helm. She left Shirati with mixed feelings..

"Some considered Somalia to be one of the worst places on earth," says Elsie. In 1971, the downtrodden nation, northeast of Kenya, bordering on the Indian Ocean remained a land of abject poverty. Bordering on salt water with few rivers and arid soil, Somalians suffered from a life-threatening lack of fresh drinking water. Little agriculture was carried on and without this sustenance many were plagued with disease. Illiteracy was epidemic.[1]

Never one to hide her opinions, Elsie gives her own assessment of the problems in the nation of Somalia thirty years past.

> All Muslim countries were poor. The drought and the climate was part of the problem, but they had poor leadership and the country was managed badly. Still they'd accept western money and assistance when they could give none back. Countries that were Muslim-led didn't hold with Christian values. They didn't treat their people in a Christian way. In fact they treated their people badly.

Given Somalia's reputation and the short-term duration of Elsie's assignment, it is perhaps surprising how quickly she leapt at the invitation to come. Much of her enthusiasm might be explained in her well-documented love of a good adventure. On the scale of challenges, Somalia would have surely ranked very high. The invitation also flattered her, and Elsie loved being loved. "The Mission Board said that I was the only person who could do the job – that I was the person they wanted. So I ended up in a place where I couldn't speak the language,

[1] With files from: Smoker, Dorothy and Merle Eshelman, MD *God Led Us to Somalia*. Salunga, Pa. Eastern Mennonite Board of Missions and Charities, 1956; "Somalia Guide-National Geographic." www.nationalgeographic.com/travel/countries/somalia-guide/; "Somalia: Maps, History, Geography, Government, Culture, Facts." www.infoplease.com/ipa/AO107979.html.

with two young nurses and I had to keep the place running." She knew though she'd have to be mindful of her "p's and q's." "I knew I had to be careful about what I said; I knew I didn't always do that, and at times it got me into a scrape or two."

Elsie stepped off the plane on the sun-baked tarmac of Mogadishu Airport. The calendar pointed to summer at home in the Northern Hemisphere, but here near the Equator it was the coolest part of the year. Still in a July letter to friends in Canada shortly after her arrival she remarks: "It's sticky and hot, but after freezing for a year in London now I'll thaw and bake."

From Mogadishu, she traveled to Jamama, 265 miles to the south, almost at the Kenyan border. Situated along the bank of the Guiba River, one of only two fresh water sources in the country, Jamama had the advantage of having two narrow greenbelts directly adjacent the river. Within 100 feet of the riverbank, the green turned to brown sand.[2] In a step-up from Shirati, Elsie would have her own house situated beside the hospital. Plain and basic, with water supplied by donkey express, Elsie was still pleased with her situation. "I immediately liked Somalia and felt I would be happy there." Still she was startled at the reception she received. "When we'd walk to the market, the young kids would throw stones at us. There were so few white people there, and they'd been taught to think of us as evil."

Jamama Hospital where Elsie would spend her days was small – only twenty-five beds, but ran full tilt. The two junior nurses, doing the work of three, maybe four, were ecstatic to see her. They dealt with the commonplace African health problems: parasites, infections, dysentery and the usual diseases of malaria and tuberculosis. Leprosy was not the widespread problem it had been in Tanzania. In the best of times, the most pressing issue at Jamama was malnutrition; at the worst, it was starvation. Children were the most vulnerable. The Somali infant mortality rate was staggering. Humanitarian aid in the form of shipments of rice, various grains and milk powder came regularly into the country.

---

[2] Interview with Rev. Victor and Mrs. Viola Dorsch, New Hamburg, July 2010.

> But very little of it got to the people who needed it the most. You went into little grocery stores and there was plenty of milk-powder for sale. It was supposed to have been given free to the starving people. It wasn't. The milk was being sold for profit.

Furious about the situation, she began going to the local market place and purchasing as much milk powder as her own meager resources could afford. She then gave every infant and child a glass of milk when they arrived at Jamama Hospital. There, Elsie and her nursing colleagues were run off their feet. She remembers a particularly torrid day with a woman in labour, another pregnant patient hemorrhaging and several being treated for injuries suffered in a serious car crash.

> In the midst of all that one of the nurses handed me a telegram. It was from my bother Howard telling me that our father had died. I looked at it and stuck it back in my pocket. I had no time to let myself think about this with what was going on around me. I remember thinking that I'd consider the news when things slowed down – and I did.

With the arrival of American Doctor Houseman, Elsie's job in Somalia was at an end. Her plan to return to Canada to work in the north would have to be put on the back burner again. She'd received another African invitation from old friend Hershey Leaman, now an administrator at the Mennonite Mission Board. It looked like she might be heading to Rusinga Island on Lake Victoria, in Kenya.

Chapter Thirty-Four
Rusinga Island

Hershey (Hersh) Leaman had come to Shirati as a Conscientious Objector, 1W classification, around the same time as Elsie. When his alternative service stint was up, he had returned to the US, and completed his education. He then returned to work with the Eastern Mennonite Board of Missions, and was now Director of their operations in Kenya. Hersh had become aware of a job opening that he thought Elsie Cressman would like.

An experienced and self-starting person was needed to start up a Health Clinic on Rusinga Island, off the north shore of Lake Victoria in Kenyan territory. Hersh had immediately thought of Elsie and sent a letter to her. From his home in Pennsylvania, he recalls what he asked of his Shirati friend:

> Knowing Elsie's strengths from her work at the Leprosarium I saw her as a good person to do the same on Rusinga. Her midwifery training and overall experience made her an excellent candidate. And her ability to take her own initiative without doctors around made her a strong person for the Rusinga position.[1]

The tenure of the Rusinga job was for three years. By this time, the Health Centre should be running smoothly and all administration could be turned over to African health care officials. Elsie was enthusiastic with what she heard, and immediately made her interest known. The job was hers and she eagerly accepted. She was heartened by the knowledge that the predominant tribe and language spoken on Rusinga was Luo. These people had made up the majority of her patients at Shirati and she had learned some of the language.

[1] Interview with Hersh Leaman, Lititz, Pennsylvania, May-June 2010.

Lying in the eastern waters of Lake Victoria, just off the mainland of Kenya, Rusinga Island[1] was indeed apart from the hustle and bustle of mainland life. Only 16 km long and 5 km wide at its widest point, Rusinga was home to 10,000 inhabitants. A ferry plied back and forth between the island and the mainland.

Most inhabitants made their living from agriculture, with millet and maize being the predominant crops grown. Fishing was abundant in the then-clean, clear waters of Lake Victoria.

Constant off-shore breezes cooled the island. This afforded it a moderate day time temperature which made swimming a pleasant pastime at the black crystalline beaches. Today Rusinga is a favourite Kenyan tourist attraction, but in the early 1970's, tourism was limited, due to poor road systems throughout the island.

Rusinga Island's main claim to fame was as the birthplace of Kenya national hero Tom Mboya. Mboya, assassinated in 1969 had been touted as the successor of Kenyan president Jomo Kenyatta. The island Health Centre bore Mboya's name.

Financing for the Health Centre had come from German sources, although it would be administered locally. Hersh Leaman had only acted as conduit to Elsie. Indeed there was no Mennonite presence in the area. The only Christian congregation was Seventh Day Adventists, who also ran a boys' school on the island.

Elsie was welcomed to the newly-opened Tom Mboya Health Care Centre by her two colleagues, both Registered Nurses. One woman was German, the other one Dutch. Several local Africans also assisted there.

As was the norm for Elsie, there was a period of adjustment between the two Europeans and herself. "At first we clashed," she says, "but we eventually learned to get along and usually worked well together."

[1] "The Mfangano-Rusinga Island Complex-UNESCO World Heritage." www.whc.unesco.org/en/tentativelists/html; "Rusinga Island:Define, Explore. Discuss." www.museumstuff.com/learn/topics/Rusinga_Island.

Each nurse had her own accommodation close to the Centre. A verandah on the front of the house was a pleasant place to sit to catch the evening breeze. But given the heavy workload, the three nurses had few leisure hours. "We were more or less on call most of the time," Elsie reports. She estimates numbers as high as 100 patients a day. Most of the cases treated were seen as outpatients although there were six to eight beds for those who needed hospitalization.

Any patients needing care that the nurses couldn't handle were transported off the island to the mainland. Occasionally when a patient couldn't be moved, a doctor would make the crossing to Rusinga. One of the nurses made regular mainland trips when drugs and medical supplies were needed.

As was the case throughout Africa, malaria was the most prevalent medical condition seen at the Health Centre. Indeed, given the moist climate of Rusinga the incidence of the disease was higher than the African average. Children and pregnant women were those most affected, and a full 35% of infant deaths on Rusinga were as a result of malaria. Pneumonia and croup were also commonly seen too.

Although modern in construction, Mboya Health Centre was lacking in equipment. Elsie and her colleagues had to often "make do." But having "made do" for almost two decades at Shirati, Elsie was a master of the art. One of her ingenious constructions was a homemade "croup tent" that helped to nurse Rusinga infants suffering from serious croup back to health.

Elsie also specialized in frontier techniques that "did in a pinch" when no other resources were available. She recalls a man being brought to the Centre after being in a serious car accident:

> I knew very little about fractures, having done none of this nursing work at Shirati. But that detail didn't matter. The patient was here and we had to do what we could. So we put him on a bed, stretched his legs out and rigged up a type of traction. His legs were crushed and while amputation wasn't necessary, they'd need to be set.

With no experience in setting bones, Elsie still rolled up her sleeves and, assisted by one of the other nurses, placed the man's two limbs in traction. This would hold until a physician, called to do the final bone setting, could arrive from the mainland. Elsie beams at the memory of the doctor's words when he saw the two nurses' handiwork:

> He looked shocked and said "you two nurses did this?" We were almost afraid to admit it because we thought he was being very critical of our work. But that was not the case. When we said we did it, he told us that he couldn't have put the two legs in traction any better than we had done.

Praise like this made Elsie glow inside and out. She also recalls a baby, "collapsed and not breathing" being rushed in for treatment. With no modern equipment at her fingertips, Elsie and one of the other nurses did basic mouth-to-mouth resuscitation until the infant began breathing again. He eventually recovered. Elsie always shone in such situations. "I loved the responsibility that was placed on my shoulders at Rusinga and I loved the independence I had. I was the one in charge, and sometimes I had to make life and death decisions."

But not all outcomes were as happy. She recalls a patient "ghostly white," a danger sign in people with black skin that their blood hemoglobin was dangerously low. "He probably could have been saved by a blood transfusion, but we had no capacity to do this with the limited equipment we had here." Helpless, they watched the man die before their eyes.

Occasionally Elsie's farm background assisted her to save a life of a different sort. In this case it was a cow.

At home, my brother Howard kept in his barn medicine cabinet, a large needle made of bone. "It's if one of the cows gets into a hayfield with fresh hay and gets bloated," he told me. He said that if this happened and the animal was in distress, you just pushed the needle into the cow's belly. The gas came out and the cow got better. I guess I filed this information somewhere.

At Shirati she'd come across a couple of bone needles and kept them, thinking that one day she'd have a use for them. At Rusinga she got her opportunity. "One of my African workers came to me and said: "My mother's cow has gotten into the cassava patch and is badly bloated. It is the only piece of property that she has and if it dies it will be a terrible hardship to her." Elsie chuckles that her mind flashed back to Howard's words, at the same time recalling the handy bone needle. "I fetched it and told the woman how to poke it right into the cow's stomach." She laughs that the woman looked surprised, but believed that if Nurse said it was so, then it was! "The next time I saw her I asked her about the cow. She smiled and said: "I pushed the needle in the stomach like you said and it went "Pop, Pop, Pop. The air came out and the cow is just fine."

By 1975, the Women's Liberation movement was changing the face of society in the West. However on secluded Rusinga Island, as was the case in much of tribal Africa, a woman's role remained virtually the same. "Women were nothing in African society;" Elsie had observed, "and they had no rights or property or say in much to do with their lives." At Shirati, Elsie learned that the cause of her patients' "immorality" often had its root in this inequity. "If a man wanted a woman, whether she was his wife or not, she had no right to say no to him."

At Rusinga, the status quo went even farther, and usually involved the all-powerful Chief of the island tribe. "If a woman went against her husband or disobeyed him in any way, the Chief could put her in jail." In principal, the strong-minded and independent Elsie found such prejudice distasteful, but she was well-aware that there was little she could do to remedy it. Still if injustice happened to a female she knew well, like one of her workers, she'd not be afraid to "stick her oar in." One day she had cause to do just that.

> I paid this woman a pittance, less than 20 shillings a month but this was all the money she had and it should have been hers. But I heard from her that her husband was taking it. Well that made me furious and I confronted him. "You take your wife's money again and you'll have to deal with me." For a while I got no more complaints

> from her, But she later told me that when she'd asked her husband to build her a new house, he'd refused saying: "Get your big nurse to build it for you!"

Used to running her own show at Shirati, Elsie took no nonsense either from the island Chief or his Councilmen if they opposed her for a needed improvement or repair for the clinic. "I had no problems standing up to them and they seemed to take it from me," she chuckles.

In an ideal world, such a role model as Elsie Cressman might have opened the door, even a crack to independence and autonomy for the women of Rusinga Island. Realistically this was not to be the case. Bound by centuries of tradition, African women led their lives as their forbearers had done—even when that meant the rituals of female circumcision. Taking on the role of midwife on Rusinga as she had done at Shirati, Elsie regularly came up against the women mutilated by this ritual.

> Pretty well all the Luo women on Rusinga had been sewn up, circumcised around age two or three. In fact, girls who were about the same age were circumcised all together. It was done as a type of party. Most of them accepted circumcision and even embraced it. I encountered a few women who, some reason, hadn't been circumcised, and they were considered outcasts by the majority who were.

The problems for medical personnel who encountered a circumcised female in late labour were significant. Before the baby could be delivered, a hasty incision had to be made in the vaginal opening. Often thick scar tissue made the surgery a difficult one. "So just as the baby was coming out, all this blood was gushing out as well," Elsie says. "Oh it was a terrible mess and women lost so much blood, when they needed their blood supply the most."

Three years passed happily on Rusinga Island, and before she knew it was time to move on. A strong foundation had been built in the running of Rusinga Island Tom Mboya Health Care Centre. It could now be turned over to African personnel. Sometime in the Fall of 1976, Elsie climbed aboard the ferry for her last trip across Lake Victoria to the mainland. Twice her plans to return permanently to Canada had been scuttled by invitations to stay in Africa. There would not be a third.

Part Five

Midwifery

Chapter Thirty-five
Finding Work

Somewhat reluctantly in the Fall of 1976, Elsie boarded a plane in Nairobi for Canada and a future that remained, for the present, unseen. Whatever path she would follow, it better have a real income. After three years living on the pittance that patients could pay when they came in for treatment at the Health Centre, Elsie was pretty well broke. Not a warm thought for a woman now well into her 50's.

She'd not lived in the Waterloo Region since she left for La Junta Colorado in 1946. But it was home and this is where she would settle. She'd have to live, at least for the immediate future, with her brother Howard and his family on the Cressman farm. Howard also lent her some money to buy a used car.

Luckily Elsie didn't need to look far or hard for work. With her three decades of nursing experience behind her, employment was as close as one of the two hospitals in the Kitchener-Waterloo area. Within days of her returning she was hired at the Kitchener-Waterloo Hospital (now Grand River). She'd be nursing on one of the hospital's medical floors.

Elsie sorely missed Africa and looked forward to invitations to show her large collection of slides from Shirati, Somalia and Rusinga. She also occasionally cooked up an African meal for missionary or church friends too and recalls making the African staple ugali and sweet African tea for Biehn Church members one Sunday after service. But ask Elsie Cressman what she missed the most about Africa during these years and she'd answer "delivering babies."

Twenty years in Africa and countless babies delivered there had only reinforced Elsie's beliefs that giving birth to babies was "a woman's natural and normal function."

> If truth be known, most women want it that way. They want to have their babies without drugs to dull the

> sensation of giving birth. And if at all possible, unless there is great risk to either the baby or the mother, they want the baby to be born vaginally, not by Cesarean section, not cut from the mother's womb.[1]

In Elsie's view, a hospital was the wrong place for a baby to come into the world:

> Hospitals are, after all, for sick people and a pregnant woman isn't sick. If a woman does give birth in a hospital, personnel there treat births technically, instead of focusing on women primarily.[2]

Home was the ideal place to bring a child into the world, Elsie knew. "There's just something warm and homey about a baby being born in the bed where the parents sleep."

As for medical doctors, especially general practitioners delivering babies, Elsie thought even less favourably. "GPs are given only very brief training in childbirth, and really don't know much about it."[3] Even obstetricians failed to impress in Elsie Cressman's books. Trained to deal with high risk, unusual births, obstetricians were "bored with normal births," she'd found.

The one most appropriate to deliver babies was the midwife. And by the time Elsie Cressman arrived back in Canada after over twenty years abroad, North American women were finally starting to see things her way.

The midwife, honoured and trusted in much of the world, had been relegated to a dubious position in mid-20th century North America. The modern woman had her babies in a hospital; she was sedated so as to experience none of the pain of childbirth. And unless complications

[1] "Mennonite Midwife on Forefront of Controversial Cause," *The Mennonite Reporter*, September 16, 1985. Vol.15, #18.

[2] Ibid.

[3] Ibid.

occurred, her babies came into the world thanks to her family doctor.

Only women whose religious beliefs rejected modernity, such as Old Order Mennonites and Amish, or those who had emigrated from Europe or Asia where midwives still commonly delivered babies favoured the midwife. By the "wild and wooly" 1960's, hippies and flower children had begun to discover the midwife. These free spirits viewed her as a link to a "natural world," not bound by conventions.

But such midwifery clients remained few, and midwives practiced in a shadowy realm, without status or recognition and carried out in the secrecy of the client's home. Nor was the Canadian midwife likely professionally-trained. Canada of the mid-century had no midwife-training institutes,[4] although several were running in the US. The best-known of these was established by pioneering midwife Mary Breckinridge in Kentucky.[5] While a few practicing Canadian midwives had been trained in Europe or the US, most were uncertified or "lay midwives." The "pickings" were slim indeed for women wishing a birth alternative, and most sacrificed preference for convenience and availability.

Such was the situation when Registered Nurse and professionally-trained midwife Elsie Cressman returned to Canada in 1976. Soon her phone began to ring.

---

[4] The Midwife Act of 1920, in the British protectorate of Newfoundland had accorded status to "lay midwives." Between 1924 and 1934 midwife training was offered at Grace Maternity Hospital in St. John's Newfoundland. This status was rescinded in 1934.

[5] Elsie's sister Ruth Cressman (Strubar) trained at Breckinridge's Frontier School of Midwifery and Family Nursing in Hyden, Kentucky. As a midwife, she attended clients in the remote Appalachian Mountains.

Chapter Thirty-Six
Starting a Little Practice

Around 1980, Elsie took a call from Kitchener-area lay midwife Mary Molnar. Mary asked if she'd like to act as a backup or second midwife for several of her births. Elsie's nurses training would be an asset. Elsie agreed and soon was helping Mary out from time to time. The demographics of Mary's clients surprised Elsie.

It wasn't Old Order Mennonite and hippies wanting midwives. It was educated women, in their early 30's working in professional jobs or with professional husbands who wanted home births. Some of them had European or British connections.

She gave some thought to setting up her own practice but felt she'd want physician back up in case of complications. In any case, if it was meant to be it would happen was Elsie's feeling. Later that year, the timing and circumstances seemed to coalesce. Elsie recalls the conditions she set for the client, her first as a primary midwife:

> I'm not sure how the woman knew who I was but she called me at home and told me that she wanted a home birth. I told her that I'd consider doing this for her but first she'd need to approach her doctor. She had to have a backup in case something went wrong and she needed to be admitted to the hospital.

The back up was essential too as the baby's due date may occur when Elsie had committed to attending a nursing conference out of the country. The woman agreed and the partnership was sealed on a handshake. "How could you have someone sign a consent contract when you're performing a service that's considered illegal?" Elsie asks, with a chuckle.

Still in thinking back to this first call for her professional services Elsie says she did not take the step lightly:

> I was well aware that practicing midwifery was not technically legal in Ontario, but of course untrained midwives had been delivering babies for certain women for hundreds of years. I knew full well that in Ontario the rules would be different than in Africa, where I had delivered babies without doctor supervision.

A few days later the woman contacted Elsie again saying she had secured a doctor backup. With this promise fulfilled, Elsie had her first midwife client. Over the progress of the woman's pregnancy, the two met regularly at Elsie's house. As the delivery date approached, Elsie reminded the woman of the potential of the delivery date conflict. "She assured me that the doctor back-up was well-secured," Elsie laughs. "Well was I wrong."

> Then, I received a letter in the mail from the woman's doctor. It was three pages of ranting about how he would never be my backup; that what I was doing was illegal. He told me in no uncertain terms what he thought of me and my kind.

The outraged letter would serve as an ominous foreshadowing of the controversy that Elsie's work would stir up over the next 25 years. It opened her eyes to the deep waters she would navigate if she chose to continue on as midwife in Ontario. Far from causing her to curtail her midwifery business, it encouraged her.

> I'd found out quickly what some doctors felt about midwives. They thought we were terrible. And do you know what? I didn't care. I decided that if women wanted me to be their midwife I would, and to heck with what the doctors thought.

Fate smiled on the drama. The night before Elsie's departure, she assisted the woman to deliver a healthy baby, at home. A sleep-deprived Elsie then caught her plane.

Chapter Thirty-Seven
Growing, Growing

Over the next months Elsie continued to take calls from women who had heard there was a "real" midwife in town. She'd started to do some team midwifery too with RN Violet Ropp. Violet had gained considerable experience in Obstetrics at St. Mary's Hospital in Kitchener before taking her Midwifery training in London, England.

While their methods and approaches occasionally clashed, the two midwives were united in philosophy. "We get so intertwined … that the woman often doesn't know who delivered," Elsie told writer Eleanor Barrington for Barrington's book *Midwifery is Catching.*[1]

Often the contact was made by personal letter. Elsie recalls one in particular from an Old Order Mennonite woman, Louisa,[2] age 27 and pregnant with her second child. Louisa had her first baby in an area hospital delivered by the family GP. It had been a difficult and stressful experience for Louisa, one she wished to avoid again. She wrote to Elsie:

> The hospital is a grand modern place, but I was afraid I wouldn't have my thoughts thankful enough towards God, being in such a different place. And at the hospital they say we're to leave our modesty at the door, and pick it up on our way out.[3]

Elsie was fully sympathetic to the wishes and beliefs of women like Louisa.

> I knew how much the thoughts of invasive hospital equipment and procedures like C-sections went against their beliefs, and I felt very good about saving them from

[1] Barrington, Eleanor. *Midwifery is Catching.* Toronto: New Canada Publications, 1985, p. 94.

[2] Only Louisa's given name is used to protect her privacy.

[3] Barrington, p. 95.

> this. If I was the way they could have the normal births that they wanted, then I would do all that I could to help them.

Privacy and distain for modernity, presented only one of the reasons why Old Order women like Louisa preferred to give birth at home. Transportation into town by horse and buggy was agonizingly slow if a woman was in active labour. The ultimate indignity for them would be to give birth before the horse reached its destination. Nor is a "buggy birth" safe. On a dark country night, a horse and buggy pulled over to the side of the road only invites tragedy.

Elsie recalls that Louisa had informed her doctor of her wish to find a midwife and his response was: "why wait nine months for a dead baby?" Undeterred, even galvanized into action by the man's reaction, Louisa searched out and eventually located Elsie. She recalls Elsie's return letter: "I wrote to her looking for advice and help and encouragement and that's what I got. I don't know what we'd have done if we couldn't get her."

Elsie drew the line with multiple births though, and told women carrying twins or triplets that they'd have to deliver in a hospital under the care of a physician. But even with these precautions, she was occasionally put in the multiple births delivery business.

> I thought that I'd made that clear with one patient who was carrying twins. But then she called me right at the time of delivery and said: "The babies are on their way right now!" What could I do? I knew she'd never have time to get by buggy to the hospital so I left right away. By the time I arrived, one of the babies was almost out and winking at me! But they were both delivered safely.

To be cautious Elsie called an ambulance to take both mother and babies to the hospital for a post-partum medical check.

As word spread both throughout the Mennonite and mainstream grapevine, about this Elsie Cressman, the calls and letters came fast and furious. She'd recently moved from the family farm in New Hamburg to her own home on Karn Avenue in Kitchener. There she'd made an office to see clients, one day a week.

By now Elsie was seeing up to ten women monthly for initial and pre-natal visits, and was averaging one to two deliveries a month. She usually was able to squeeze them in between her nursing duties at the hospital. But when they occurred during her shifts she switched them with colleagues.

Things were hectic but Elsie was in heaven. She'd have given up the nursing position in a minute but it paid the bills. Still she wondered if she might, someday, be able feed herself and pay her mortgage on a midwife's salary.

A chance meeting with a powerful advocate would start her down this path.

Chapter Thirty-Eight
A Powerful Advocate

Former Director of Nursing at Kitchener's Conestoga College, Pat Legault says she was an "oddball" in her field, for the times.[1] From the time she assumed her position in the mid-1970's, until her retirement 20 years later, Nursing Director Legault's attitude towards midwifery was unconventional, to say the least.

> After I'd left home in Ontario, I'd nursed for a while in a small hospital in BC. There were fewer boundaries between disciplines there. Specialists in Gynecology helped out OB's; rheumatologists assisted cardiologists. In general, staff helped each other out all the time, whether it was in their field or not.
>
> So when I got back to Ontario I had to re-adjust to the idea of "specialists" – specially-trained professionals doing one job and only that job. The idea that only physicians – GPs and later obstetricians – delivering babies was a bit restrictive to me.

Pat and her siblings had also been born at home with a midwife, an event that predisposed her to midwives' efficiency and practicality. But in the medical circles where she worked and traveled, she kept her views to herself – mostly.

Early in 1981, she'd heard about "this Mennonite midwife," Elsie Cressman who was delivering babies for area women who wanted homebirths. "Elsie wasn't very popular with the medical establishment, for sure," she recalls. Pat hoped she'd get the chance to meet Elsie, a

[1] Interview with Pat Legault.September, 2009.

woman she thought was "brave to be doing what she believed in."

Pat got her chance one night during a panel discussion on birth which she had organized for the Registered Nurses Association of Ontario (RNAO). Bucking popular tastes, Pat had insisted that Midwifery be part of the panel discussion. In the audience was Elsie, a Registered Nurse, as well as trained Midwife. The two met and exchanged pleasantries.

On Elsie's part, she immediately sensed an ally from an unlikely corner – mainstream medicine. From Pat's perspective, Elsie presented a woman bucking the mainstream, despite criticisms. "I immediately wanted to support her in some way," Pat recalls. Little did she imagine that she would have the opportunity so soon.

In September 1981, Elsie found a letter in her mailbox.[1] It bore the letterhead of the College of Nurses of Ontario. The writer was Joan MacDonald, the organization's Executive Director. MacDonald reported that she had been informed by Dr. Michael Dixon, Registrar of The College of Physicians and Surgeons of Ontario that two midwives, Elsie Cressman and Violet Ropp were "practicing illegally somewhere in the Waterloo area."

As proof of his charge, Dixon had forwarded to Macdonald a copy of the introductory letter that Ropp and Cressman gave to prospective clients. (Dixon does not reveal how he has come into possession of the letter but asks Macdonald to investigate.) MacDonald requests both of them to "arrange to come in to discuss this ... at your convenience." Needing some advice, Elsie decided to call Pat Legault.

Pat recalls the situation:

> Elsie and Violet were not breaking any law by delivering babies in the homes of their clients. But I still encouraged them to take the opportunity of meeting with MacDonald to gather more information.

Elsie attended the meeting herself, and soon became aware that MacDonald's letter had no basis in law. It had been sent in an effort to

[1] All references are to a series of letters between Joan MacDonald, Executive Director of the College of Nurses of Ontario and Elsie Cressman, Midwive. September 1981-January 1982. Files from Elsie Cressman.

scare the two women into closing their business. Little did MacDonald, or Dixon know who they were dealing with! Elsie left the meeting as firmly convinced that the two organizations had not a leg to stand on in their bravado. "Violet and I had taken midwife training; we were both qualified nurses and we were delivering babies with the consent of the mother in the privacy of her own home."

The exchange of letters, which continued over the next few months, indicates that neither side was willing to give. In one MacDonald-penned letter to Violet Ropp, she threatens that continuation of midwifery services "could place your registration as a Nurse in jeopardy." A later one, to both women charges that "failure to respond promptly will necessitate more formal action under the Health Disciplines Act." Subsequently MacDonald insists that the College of Nurses "must have some assurance" that the two will ensure that "every client be under the care of a physician."

At this point, Pat decides to ghost-write a written response on behalf of Elsie and Violet:

> Today an increasing number of persons are giving much thought to the manner in which the birth of their children is handled. Many of these individuals have strong feelings for natural, un-medicated births. They often insist on birthing in a home atmosphere. The nurse with specialized training in midwifery has an unusually important role here ...

Determined to counter the College of Nurses using their own language, Legault then skillfully quotes several paragraphs from their Standards of the College of Nurses:

> Nursing is a discipline concerned with the promotion of the well-being of the individual in society. Inherent in nursing is the respect for the dignity, worth, autonomy and individuality of each human being.

Pat, Elsie and Violet now sit back to see in what direction the fur will now fly. It comes less than a month later. A late December 1981 letter from Toronto arrives, informing the midwives that the matter has been "turned over to the College of Physicians and Surgeons of Ontario for their information."

Women of lesser spunk may have buckled, but encouraged by Pat Legault, Elsie remained resolute. Indeed she seemed to grow stronger as the battle is dragged out. She writes:

> It seems impossible to ignore the very strong feelings of those people (parents) for natural, un-medicated births. This to them is extremely important to their health and happiness...and if we ignore these requests for help, we will be violating the standards of the College of Nurses in respecting the dignity and worth of each human being.

Elsie's words fell on deaf ears. In a David vs. Goliath letter from MacDonald of January 1982, The College of Nurses advises Elsie Cressman, RN and Violet Ropp, RN of "the possibility of being charged with the illegal practice of medicine."

Then the letters stop! The January 26 letter marks the end of the war of words between the College of Nurses of Ontario (and their silent partner The College of Physicians and Surgeons), Elsie Cressman and Violet Ropp. No more letters follow. Pat Legault speculates on the reason:

> Times were changing and I'd like to think that from my place in the nursing hierarchy, I helped change it. I'd done lots of talking about midwifery to both the Registered Nurses Association and the College of Nurses and how we as nurses had to embrace it. And I think they were slowly coming round to the same point of view.

She also believes that around this time, leadership at the College of Nurses changed with a less "hard-line" Executive Director taking the helm from Joan MacDonald.

Whatever the reason, the College of Nurses of Ontario backed down. And while the stand taken by the mainstream medical hierarchy seems "much ado about nothing," by today's standards, the letters form an important historic backdrop to the changing times for midwifery. Elsie herself chuckles at the memory of the brou-ha-ha:

> I was never worried about this you know, because I knew that nothing was going to happen. It was all just words. Violet and I were never charged and we went on doing what we were doing. Why? Because women wanted it.

Chapter Thirty-Nine
The St. Jacobs Birthing Home

By now Elsie's phone was steadily ringing with prospective clients. In 1983, she cut back her hours at the hospital to devote more time to her midwifery clients. The money earned by delivering babies didn't match her hospital salary by a long shot, but Elsie was OK. "I always was able to live on next to nothing at all." Calls also came from other midwives wanting to work with her. Elsie was glad for the relief and began to wonder if she should take her "on-the-side" midwifery business a step further and open her own practice.

She had lots of support for that. Midwife supporters had been pushing for a local clinic, a place where Elsie could see her clients and where various childbirth-centred classes such as Pre-Natal, Exercise or Nutrition might be held. Taking it a step further, dreamers dreamed of a real Birthing Home, an alternative to the woman's house or the hospital as a birthing place. Realistically, given the medical prejudice against midwifery in Ontario this was just a "pipe dream."

Elsie herself liked the idea. It would mean a lot of work but what idea, worth its salt wasn't? She decided to make a phone call to friend Pat Legault to see what she thought of the notion. Maybe it was do-able after all. Pat recalls their conversation:

> Elsie wondered if I might be interested in sitting on a committee that was being formed to investigate the possibility of beginning a Birthing Home in St. Jacobs. She told me that she'd felt a growing amount of support for such a place. This was music to my ears.

Pat eagerly jumped on board, "although I was very careful to let my superiors know what I was up to," she recalls. "I could also never encroach on working time with something like this, and I was fully aware of how far I could and couldn't go."

Summer 1983 saw a number of midwifery supporters coming together for the first planning meeting for the proposed St. Jacobs Family Birthing Home. The group's goal was a loose one initially: "to assess the viability of beginning a Midwifery (Birthing) Home to provide whatever prenatal and postnatal education, care and support for women and their families as possible under present laws."[1]

The first step saw a Board Executive named. While Pat Legault was the obvious choice to head the committee, given her professional credentials in the medical "mainstream," she initially held off.[2] "I knew the limits, given my occupation. So I volunteered instead to be Secretary for the group."

Businessman Bill Noonan of Cambridge took the lead position on the committee. Other Board members were: Libby Noonan, Phil and Anne Shantz, Fae Knott, Milo Shantz, Gordon Smith, Ankara Robinson, and Elsie Cressman.

Noonan had some political connections, one being then-Progressive Conservative Minister of Health Larry Grossman. In conversation with Grossman one day, Bill had mentioned the work that was going on in St. Jacobs. He also floated the idea of a "Birthing Centre," as an alternative to home or hospital births. Grossman looked horrified and warned the startled Noonan that it would be over his "dead body" that such a facility would be on his watch as Health Minister. Noonan reported to the Board that it was unlikely their dream would ever receive validation under any Progressive Conservative government.[3]

Finding a suitable location for the St. Jacobs project was tops on the Board's agenda. When the manse at St. Jacobs Mennonite Church became vacant, it was rented. On September 15, 1984, the St. Jacobs Family Birthing Home officially opened.

One room served as Elsie's office and examining room; others were rented to various midwifery-friendly clients. The La Leche

---

[1] *The Update*, Newsletter of the St. Jacobs Family Birthing Home, September 1983.

[2] Pat Legault eventually became Chair of the St. Jacobs Family Birthing Home's Board of Directors.

[3] Interview with Pat Legault, September 2009.

League held information sessions and classes there, as did pre-natal teacher Ankara Robinson; pre-natal nutrition expert Cecily Alexander and Heather Jones' natural family planning classes. The St. Jacob's Mennonite Church was now "hopping" seven days a week.

Each Thursday afternoon was designated "Elsie day" when she would see clients. The small waiting room was crowded with mothers-to-be, their husbands or partners, children and extended family. Elsie encouraged them all to be part of the midwifery experience.

With no government funding to support the Home financially, fundraising would ensure its survival. Volunteers, many of them Elsie's present and former clients were essential in this respect and they planned a never-ending round of bake sales, raffles and teas. On her "shoestring" salary, Elsie volunteered a portion of her midwifery fees to be put towards rent.

A quarterly newsletter, *The Update*, edited by Board Member Judy McMullan kept supporters apprised of developments both at the local centre and at other similar initiatives going on in the province. And by 1984, the midwifery pot was surely bubbling, not just in little St. Jacobs, but across Ontario.

Chapter Forty
The Long Road to Legislation

Shortly after Elsie Cressman began practicing in 1981, a group of Ontario midwives and nurse-midwives banded together to form the Association of Ontario Midwives (AOM).[1] This was the first step in what would become an almost two-decade-long march to legalization of the midwifery profession in the province. At the same time, citizens groups similar to the St. Jacobs organization were coming together.

Pro-midwifery movements at the grass roots level were also occurring across Canada. In 1983, the Midwifery Coalition of Nova Scotia was formed. Similar movements were occurring in the Prairies concurrently. British Columbia had led the way a decade earlier.

Midwifery moved into the legal system in 1982, with a high-profile Kitchener inquest.[2] The courts were hearing circumstances of the death of a midwife-delivered infant. Judgment handed down at the conclusion of the case that midwifery be legislated, had advocates clicking their heels together in joy.

The Quebec legislature would be the first Canadian house of government to entertain dialogue on the midwifery movement. There in 1983, a government paper *Accoucher ou Se Fair Coucher* (To Deliver or Be Delivered) presented arguments, pro and con for government-funded midwife services. It was the "kick-start" midwife activists needed to begin intense lobbying of government for their cause. The same year an NDP Private Member's bill[3] presented in the Ontario legislature proposed the legalization of midwifery. It also

[1] With files from: Benoit, Cecilia, *Reconceiving Midwifery.* McGill-Queen's University Press. 2004; Bourgeault, Ivy Lynn. *Push: the Struggle for Midwifery in Ontario.* McGill-Queen's University Press, 2006; De Vries, Raymond, *Birth by Design: Pregnancy, Maternity Care and Midwifery in North America and Europe.* Routledge Press, 2001.

[2] Ritz, Jean. "Inquest into the Death of..." May 20, 21 and June 18, 1982. Kitchener, Coroner Jack Burger. Chief Coroner's Office of Ontario.

[3] Bill 48, "An Act to Establish Midwifery as a Self-Governing Profession," Legislature of Ontario, First Reading, April 26, 1984.

recommended midwifery services be funded by the Ontario's public health plan (OHIP). While the motion was easily and swiftly defeated in the legislature, it served notice that the midwifery cause was no longer to be dismissed.

To achieve their desired outcome, Ontario advocates knew that a more powerful, organized and dedicated form of advocacy would be necessary. To this end, the consumer-led Midwife Task Force of Ontario (MTF-O) was formed in 1984. Advocates mounted an effective campaign of letter writing, public education and fund-raising. Submissions from midwifery advocates across the province were invited as well.

Acquiescing to the growing public clamour, in 1984 the Ontario Progressive Conservative government set up the Health Professions Legislation Review of Ontario (HPLRO). This board would review the delivery of all health care in the province, including that provided by midwives. The formation of HPLRO was lauded by midwife lobbies, and they moved into high gear, preparing briefs and presentations to the Board.

Integral to the HPLRO's deliberations was a paper presented jointly by the Association of Midwives and the Midwife Task Force. While at this stage liquid, the document would serve as the germ by which the future College of Midwives would determine their tenets and policies. Goals drafted included:

- integration of midwifery into the health system;
- self-regulation of the midwifery profession as distinct from nursing and medicine;
- access for midwives to both hospital and home birth settings;
- public funding for midwife services;
- multiple routes for entry into the practice, nursing not being a requirement

Government reaction to the report was guarded at best. Influenced by the powerful physician lobby, it was tabled for "future deliberations." In layman's terms, this meant "delay." Midwifery proponents were demoralized but undeterred, and lobbying continued unabated.

Hope flourished again with new Liberal Health Minister Murray Elston's announcement in April 1986 that the Ontario government was committed to legalizing midwifery and integrating it into the Ontario health system. The details of when this cataclysmic event would occur, were absent from Minister Elston's pronouncement. The first step in this lengthy process would be the formation of the Task Force on Implementation of Midwifery in Ontario (TFIMO). The government invited submissions to this fact-finding initiative.

A number of victories followed on the heels of the formation of the Task Force. The first was an announcement from the Ontario Association of Registered Nurses declaring themselves in favour of recognizing midwifery. A "reformist" group, representing 150 Ontario physicians followed suit. Both parties agreed that midwives should be independent of both the College of Physicians and Surgeons, and the College of Nurses.

The bandwagon was surely rolling, and bound to roll faster as it gained momentum.

Chapter Forty-One
Inspiring Total Confidence

Elsie followed little of the political movement that was swirling around her. Not that she wasn't keenly interested in the inroads midwifery was making on the social and political landscape, or that she was befuddled by politics. It was just that Elsie Cressman was busy ... delivering babies. Still there was much more to this baby deliverer, this understated Mennonite woman than met the eye.

Conservative in appearance, wearing the traditional female head-covering and caped dress, and plain in speaking manner, she was in reality an anomaly among her conservative Mennonite women peers. She'd earned a Registered Nursing Diploma, and a university degree in Science.

Over her twenty years nursing in Africa, she also developed an expertise in many medical matters; she understood disease and treatment. Calm and even in bearing and speech, she gave off a confidence without cockiness; a forthrightness without being overbearing. It would have been the rare woman, meeting Elsie Cressman for the first time, who would not have been impressed with her.

Andrea Horst, now Practice Administrator of the St. Jacobs Midwives Clinic first met Elsie at a church meeting around 1985. Elsie had recently resigned from her position as a nurse at the Kitchener-Waterloo Hospital to practice midwifery full-time. Andrea was hoping to have a second baby after a bad experience with her first. She recalls the circumstances:

> Elsie had been invited by our church group to do a talk and show her Africa slides. Her slides were in a bit of

> a jumble and her speech wasn't well-prepared. In any other person it would have been a disaster. But Elsie just exuded a calm, cool confidence, and I was immediately drawn to her.[1]

Included in Elsie's slides of leprosy patients at Shirati were images of happy, smiling, African mothers giving birth to healthy babies. The photos struck home with Andrea. "I'd had an unfortunate experience with my first baby, delivered with forceps in a hospital. I questioned that if these mothers could enjoy childbirth, then why couldn't I?"

After the church meeting, Andrea went home and asked her husband Brent: "What would you think if I told you I wanted a midwife to deliver our next child?" Brent answered her: "as long as the baby isn't born at home." The two look back on this conversation and laugh.

When Andrea subsequently became pregnant, one of the first calls she made was to Elsie. She had questions about homebirths as opposed to those in hospital. She recalls Elsie's manner of answering these questions:

> It was clear that having a home birth was Elsie's preference, but she never forced her beliefs on you. But she did have a way of leading you to a point of view that was shared by her. And she did it in a way that made you think that it was all your idea.

Over the next eight months the Horsts' faith in Elsie grew.

First how could anyone overlook the number of babies that she'd delivered in Africa. Plus she'd gone to school just to learn how to deliver babies! Family physicians didn't have nearly that.

By the time Andrea and Brent's second baby was delivered in 1986, both were on the St. Jacobs Family Birthing Home bandwagon. Soon, they had joined the Board of Directors and Andrea eventually took on the position of Birthing Home receptionist. She became its Practice Administrator in 1995.

---

[1] Interview with Brent and Andrea Horst, July 2009.

Chapter Forty-Two
Work and a Rest

The increased prominence that midwives received as a result of lobbying, from the Task Force and Legislation Review Committees was a double-edged sword for over-worked ones like Elsie Cressman. As the New Year of 1986 opened, she remained the only official midwife serving the St. Jacobs Family Birthing Home. Elsie was now 63 years of age.

Word of her skills had spread well beyond Waterloo Region borders. She was now traveling hours a-field to deliver babies. Elsie recalls a particularly torrid string of births that stretched her to the limit.

> I got called for a delivery in Ancaster, and just finished that when my pager went off. One of my clients in London was in labour. So I headed right there. But it was a false alarm, and she wasn't due right yet. So I turned around and headed home to Kitchener. I was almost at my house when the pager went again. It was my London mother again. She really was in labour this time so I turned around to London again and arrived in time to deliver the baby
>
> I'd now been awake for over 36 hours and thought I should catch a bit of sleep before I returned to KW. So I tried to sleep in the client's basement on her couch. No luck. It was just as well because I got a surprise page from a client in Hamilton who was quite early. I hadn't expected to see her for a couple of weeks. So I packed up my things and headed to Hamilton, delivered the baby and finally headed home.

Elsie believes that this ended her four-day sleepless marathon. "It was almost too much for me, but if I hadn't loved what I was doing so much, it would have been too stressful." Elsie always managed.

Even workhorses need a holiday, and Elsie did this in 1986. She took a month-long trip to Africa. "I thought that ten years after I left Africa was a good anniversary to return," she says. Accompanying her was her niece Evelyn, and nephews Brian and Steven. Tops on Elsie's list was a visit to Shirati.

As their vehicle neared the familiar Shirati compound, Elsie could hardly contain her excitement at seeing old friends and former patients. She wasn't disappointed as she was greeted as the treasured friend she was.

Her group would be put up in one of the new guesthouses on the property and she looked forward to seeing what improvements had been made at the "old place." An unpleasant surprise waited her inside.

> It was a shock to discover that there still were no modern toilet facilities in the guesthouse. It was just the hole in cement with a chain that released the water to flush the waste down the hole. I wasn't expecting this and as I was now in my mid-60's, with a bad hip, it wasn't pleasant or easy to accomplish.

Brian complained about the inconvenience to an official and they were able to use the modern facilities in another building. The second surprise came with the light – or lack of it.

> There was electricity installed in the guesthouse but it didn't come on till night time and then not all the time. They had diesel back-up when the power was down but then they'd run out of diesel. So we sat in the dark for the first few days until someone noticed we needed a light and gave us an Aladdin lantern.

The people part of the visit made up for the technical shortcomings. Many of the leprosy patients whom Elsie had helped during her years were still living on the compound and they were overjoyed to see her. One of her more memorable visits was to the home of the African to whom she had sold her trusty Mauser rifle. When the gun was brought out from storage, nephew Brian noticed that it still held a bullet. "Brian thought it was safer to take it out, so he did and threw the bullet away," she laughs.

She also was able to visit with her former ward Jerosa, now a mother of a baby girl. Elsie presented Jerosa with a dress and some fabric to make a garment for her daughter. A disappointment was not being mobile enough to travel to the site of the old Leprosarium, still a bumpy three miles down a dirt road from the main Shirati compound. By now Elsie's hip was causing her great pain and walking was an effort.

After several days at Shirati, the party carried on for a brief visit to Rusinga Island. Then it was on to South Africa to see more of the sights of Africa.

Chapter Forty-Three
Melissa's Tribute

Not all the cheering about midwives was coming from the increasingly vocal midwife lobby. Individual parents celebrating the midwife-delivered birth of a child were telling their stories too. And in southern Ontario, many of these stories were about Elsie Cressman.

Melissa Dennison of Kitchener shares hers:

> In 1986 it was mostly Mennonite women or hippies who were having babies at home (purposely). I am not a Mennonite woman, nor was I a hippie, but I did want a home birth, delivered by a midwife.
>
> The idea of having a hospital birth was an extremely frightening one to me. I imagined that I would lose control of the event and be forced into having an episiotomy and clinicians would use forceps to pull the baby from me...or worse.
>
> I don't remember how or when I learned of Elsie, but the moment I met her, I liked her and knew I wanted her to 'catch' my baby. I was in awe of her calmness, her humour, that wise and knowing smile, and her easy manner with all people in her presence.
>
> Over the course of my pregnancy, our visits to Elsie were a pleasure. She spent loads of time with us, fielding questions and asking many of her own. We were confident and ready for the adventure ahead.
>
> My labour went very well. I managed it successfully and delivered an eight pound beautiful boy in the bedroom of our home. The sun was just rising and beginning to shine

in the window. My husband, mother and mother-in-law were all in attendance (as well as Elsie and her partner at the time, Francesca).

But this is where things get a little fuzzy for me ... There was something "irregular" about the cord when my husband cut it. Elsie tried massage and an injection of syntocinon (a labour inducing medication) to help me expel the placenta, but the cord just broke away in her hands. Elsie tried to extract the placenta with her hands, but it was just too painful for me. The bleeding increased and my placenta would not deliver. I was slipping in and out of consciousness.

Elsie called the ambulance and the hospital to alert them of our arrival. She explained that she would not be welcomed at the hospital and that we would be treated better if she did NOT accompany us. My pulse was weak and almost non-existent by the time we arrived at the hospital. I was attended and remained there for several days. But during that time all of my worst fears about being in the hospital were confirmed.

Once it was known I had had a midwife birth, the hospital staff treated me differently than the other new mothers. They talked about me within my earshot and sent disapproving glances my way. In the Post Partum Unit, the other three new moms sharing the room with me were calling out for pain medication while their babies lay in bassinettes in the nursery down the hall. I spent the night sitting in a chair in the nursery curled up with my son because he was not allowed in the room overnight (he might disturb the sleep of the other moms).

I left the hospital before the physician was comfortable discharging me. That was only because Elsie had promised to come to my home and check in on me each day for the first week.

Melissa's relationship with Elsie continued into her second pregnancy.

> In 1991 when I became pregnant with my second child, home birth was not an option for me, given the events of my first. Elsie helped me find a physician who would support her participation in my care and one who would allow her to attend the hospital birth (as a companion only!).
>
> Elsie did research within her circles and recommended natural supplements and foods that were believed to produce healthy cords and placentas as well as babies! She recommended that I drink a concoction which consisted of castor oil and orange juice whipped frothy "with love and care by Elsie!"
>
> As time passed it was apparent that this pregnancy would be more difficult than my first. This baby's position was 'posterior' so Elsie tried (unsuccessfully) to turn him. Imagine leaning against the wall and standing on your head while in labour! We all knew this was going to be a difficult labour and delivery, but we were determined to deliver naturally.
>
> At 7:00 AM the next morning we arrived at the hospital. Elsie accompanied us as our doula, (childbirth coach), given that she had no official status as midwife. When my hospital staff discovered that the baby was in the posterior position, one RN announced: "This patient needs an epidural and a forceps rotation!"

We were upset and fearful. Elsie however remained calm and assured us that neither the baby nor me was in distress. And there was no reason we couldn't move forward with our plan to deliver without intervention.

When the second stage of labour started, Elsie could see that I was pushing very hard without getting good results. She asked the physician if she could assist me by entering the birth canal during the next contraction to determine if the baby's head was stuck on the cervix. He agreed.

She worked her magic and within minutes my baby's head was crowning. With Elsie's assistance I successfully delivered a healthy nine pound baby boy. A healthy cord and placenta came too! We only had to stay in hospital for a few hours before being released.

In the early years when I attended fund-raisers for the St. Jacobs Family Birthing Home, Elsie would always introduce me as "The only Mom she ever came close to losing."

I am grateful for the gift of Elsie Cressman and the very important role she played in the birth of my children. I am fortunate to have two very healthy, successful, productive and loving children to brag about and share with the world!

Chapter Forty-Four
New Government; Renewed Commitment

Women's rights advocates sang from the rooftops with the results of the provincial election of September 6, 1990. The New Democratic Party, led by Bob Rae swept to a majority government. New Premier Rae set the tone for the next five years with his acceptance speech. Calling Ontario "Toryland," Rae accused the long-ruling Progressive Conservatives of creating a social climate where "women and people of colour" were not welcome.[1]

Rae's government pledged to change all that. He began by naming social activist and women's rights champion Frances Lankin as his first Minister of Government Services and Chair of the Management Board of the Cabinet. After a strong showing in that portfolio, Lankin was promoted to Minister of Health in 1991.[2]

Social policies from Lankin's Ministry came fast and furious over the coming months, including the ambitious "Affirmative Action" bill. This forward-thinking initiative pledged to improve the numbers of women, non-whites and disabled in the workplace. Several anti-poverty initiatives were then initiated, including an immediate 7% increase in social assistance.

The decade-long push towards legislation of midwives received an injection of energy from Lankin's Ministry. The government celebrated the Second Reading of the Health Regulations Act in the Legislature on May 31, 1991. In a lengthy and emotional speech, Health Minister Lankin rose in the House to present the words of her government on the accomplishment:

> The Midwifery Act included in this legislative package

[1] "Bob Rae-enotes.com Reference," www.enotes.com/topic Bob_Rae.

[2] Hyland-Byrne Lesley, "Feminists in Power: Women Cabinet Ministers in NDP Government of Ontario, 1990-1995," *Policy Studies Journal*, vol. 25, 1997.

> gives legal recognition to midwives. This reversal in policy is largely due to the efforts of hundreds of individual women and a smaller number of practicing midwives who through public education, lobbying and education of other health professionals demonstrated the need and the consumer demand for midwives. Thanks to them, women will soon have the choice of obtaining care from a midwife, a choice available to women virtually everywhere except in Canada.

She went on to chide those who stood in the way of legislation and praised those "who laboured long and hard" to see it enacted:

> It should not have been so difficult for these women to bring about change, and it should not have taken so long. That it did take so long demonstrates the lack of input women and indeed the entire public have had in the health care system. People ought to have a say in the kind of health care they get and how health care is provided to them. With this legislation, which will make future policy-making flexible to change and be responsive to public opinion, it will be possible for their voices to be heard.

Lankin closed with a personal comment:

> I was thinking how remarkable this actually is, that we are finally moving to a point in time where we will have legalized midwifery in this province and show leadership in Canada in terms of establishing the practice of midwifery and the support for that profession. I think of it myself in personal terms as a young woman who has yet to have her first child. I hope I will have that opportunity in my life and I hope I will be able to have that opportunity to choose to have a child in my home with the assistance of a midwife. I am thrilled that that prospect may become a reality for me and for many other

women in this province.

Even at this stage of its evolution, advocates and detractors of the legalization of midwifery still debated its merits. Still they knew its inevitability.[1]

But a surprise midwifery pronouncement made by Minister Lankin in London Ontario, six months after Second Reading took even those in the midwifery "know" off guard.

On September 26, 1992, Health Minister Francis Lankin, keynote speaker at the First Canadian Conference on Birth Centres sent waves of excitement through the audience (waves that later became "tidal" in the medical establishment) when she announced:

> I am so delighted today to tell you that we will, before the end of the fiscal year, issue Request for Proposals to establish three community-based Birthing Centers in our province. [1]

Lankin went on to note that: "the medical profession must stop looking at childbirth as a pathology or illness, presided over by a doctor." She also warned them that they would no longer be "front line providers of this aspect of medical care." Summing up her comments, Lankin promised that the philosophical shift initiated by the soon-to-come Regulated Health Professional Act, and now the introduction of Free Standing Birthing Centres (FSBC) would put "women, not the person who is 'catching the baby' i.e. the family physician or obstetrician, fully in control of their birth process."

Lankin went on to offer, optimistically, (many would say naively) that she hoped that the three selected Birthing Centres would be open for business when legislation was enacted in fifteen months.

In a comment that came back to haunt the capable but "rosy-spectacled" Health Minister, Lankin noted that she did not expect the

[1] Speech of Health Minister Frances Lankin at the First Canadian Conference on Birth Centres, London Ontario, September 26, 1992.

medical establishment to oppose this plan. She could not have been more wrong. The response to the Minister's London announcement came with fervour.

Writing in the Canadian Medical Association Journal (CMAJ) six months after Lankin's "bombshell," journalist Cameron Johnston reflected on the Health Minister's plans from the perspective of the medical establishment. "She had introduced a prescription so radical, so unlike anything any Health Minister had attempted before, that many doctors in Canada may eventually be affected."[1]

Johnson then went on to review the verdict of Lankin's announcements from various corners of the medical establishment. From Dr. Claud Renaud, Director of Professional Affairs of the Family Physicians of Ontario came the stinging comment:

> We believe that the midwife is a new health professional who offers episodic care. It is the family doctor who should be the primary caregiver, since it is the family doctor who has the means to offer the continuity of care that patients need.[2]

The Canadian Hospital Association, representing 1200 hospitals across Canada was no more complimentary. It offered that "in all but exceptional circumstances" birthing homes were "ill-advised." The CHA agreed only that "in more remote rural areas" there might be reason but "this need does not exist in urban areas of the province."[3]

At the other end of the continuum, organizations such as the St. Jacobs Family Birthing Home reacted with unbridled glee to Frances Lankin's London announcement. They could hardly wait to find out more.

---

[1] Johnston, Cameron, "Ontario's Birthing Centre Concept May Have Impact on Hospitals. MDs Say," *The Canadian Medical Association Journal*, March 15, 1993, 148: 1004-1006.

[2] Ibid.

[3] Ibid.

Chapter Forty-Five
More Elsie Tales

It was nothing for Elsie to hop in her car, midwife kit bag at the ready, and head off to parts distant across Ontario to deliver babies. East to Toronto and the Niagara Peninsula; north as far as Sudbury; west to London and southwest to Chatham were all in her territory. Most might have drawn the line at Bolivia in South America, but not Elsie the roving midwife. She tells the story:

> The pregnant woman was a friend of a friend of mine. The woman had moved to Bolivia to do mission work with MCC. I had delivered several of my friend's babies and I guess her Bolivian friend wanted me and nobody but me to deliver her first child. Well why not? I'd use the trip as a holiday too so I didn't feel too bad about paying my own way.
>
> I got as far as the airport in Miami when they told me I couldn't go to South America because I didn't have a Visa. Well was I mad! I'd checked about this at home and was told I didn't need one. Somebody sure steered me wrong. Now here I was in an airport at night with the plane leaving and I couldn't get on. I'd have to wait until the next day to apply for my Visa in an office in downtown Miami.
>
> So I made myself a bed in the airport lounge and lay down to try to get some sleep. I put myself close to the desk so that they'd see me and feel sorry for me or something. Sleeping in uncomfortable places was nothing new to me.
>
> But a gentleman who saw me was bothered enough about

> a 60-ish Mennonite woman sleeping on her coat, to come over and suggest that there was a visitor's hostel nearby that would put me up for the night.
>
> Thanks but no thanks! I decided that I was going to stay right smack dab in front of the ones who hadn't let me board the plane! They weren't going to forget about me! Oh was I seething, and worried too. What if my client had her baby while I was curled up in the Miami airport?
>
> Anyway, I did sleep and the next morning I got myself to the Visa office. Maybe the airline had called ahead because the document was issued to me right away. No problems. Luckily I got right on a departing plane, and was finally on my way to South America.

Good fortune was with Elsie again, as the baby had waited for the Canadian midwife.

A trip to Chatham to the home of Doug and Colleen Smith around the same time was much less eventful for Elsie. Colleen recalls, with affection, her association with Elsie Cressman during the birth of her daughter, Meredith in 1986:

> I always thought having a midwife would be a wonderful thing to do, but in the days before the internet existed, I had no way of knowing where you would find one. I didn't even know if such a service existed in Canada.
>
> I gave birth to two sons, one in 1980 and the second in 1982, which were both hospital births. Even though my sons were healthy, both of the hospital births were not very satisfying experiences. I heard that midwives did practice in Canada and I learned the name of an excellent one, Elsie Cressman. When I became pregnant again, I

contacted Elsie and made arrangements to meet with her in St. Jacobs.

I was immediately impressed with Elsie's credentials and experience and most of all her warm and caring personality. She explained what she could do for us and stipulated that I must inform my family doctor that I planned to have a home birth. If there was a need for me to be transferred to the hospital, then he must agree to come and attend me there. She gave us her resume to show to him too.

I was quite nervous, wondering what my doctor's reaction would be. He read over Elsie's resume and although he didn't agree with home births, he said that if I needed to go to the hospital, he'd attend me.

My husband and I always went together to my pre-natal visits with Elsie, more than a two hour drive from home. We found her very thorough, and her calm nature always filled me with confidence. She was also knowledgeable about nutrition, and gave me a diet, rich in nutrients and vitamins which she wanted me to follow. One of the things she recommended was drinking a raspberry tea, which I was not particularly fond of, but I persevered!

A month or so before the delivery, Elsie visited our home so that she would know exactly where she was coming. I'm sure it was also to satisfy herself that our home was of a standard of cleanliness and order to welcome a home birth.

Elsie had given us instructions on how to prepare our bed for the delivery. We were to make the bed as usual with sheets, then cover this with a plastic protective sheet (or shower curtain), then cover the bed again with another set of bedding/sheets. In this way, once the birth was over, the soiled sheets and protective cover could be taken off, leaving you with a freshly made bed. Smart thinking!

The next morning, I started to feel the telltale signs of a beginning labour, so I started to get things in order. Labour progressed slowly and by about 9:00 PM that night my husband urged me to call Elsie. She said she would start out right away, even though I felt nowhere close to birth.

I rested and Elsie arrived somewhere after 11:00 PM. She did a quick internal examination and determined that I was not close, although I was definitely in labour. She suggested I go to bed and try to sleep. She laid down on our sofa and rested herself.

Around 4:00 AM, I felt very restless and my husband went downstairs to get Elsie. Our daughter was born at 5:25 AM. I cannot explain how calm Elsie made me feel during the birth, except to say that her calmness set the tone.

After Elsie had completed caring for me and our baby, she sat at the kitchen table writing up her report and having muffins and juice. Then, she got another call saying that another mom was in labour and her presence was needed. She left us with verbal and written instructions on care for me and our daughter, and followed up with phone calls later that day and for the next few days.

All in all, it was a wonderful experience being cared for by Elsie. We had complete and total trust in her, her abilities and her experience, and are forever grateful to her.

Chapter Forty-Six
Big Plans in St. Jacobs

"Delirium" might best describe the reaction in St. Jacobs to Minister Lankin's Free-Standing Birthing Centre announcement. The official St. Jacobs Family Birthing Home's reaction was recorded in the December, 1992 issue of their newsletter, *Update*.

> There is certainly no need to tell you that the St. Jacobs Family Birthing Home will be among those submitting proposals for a Free-Standing Birthing Centre, to the Ministry of Health. We will be working hard on budget projections and expect to do survey and statistics collections. We are most interested in hearing our clients' ideas and suggestions, and encourage you to write or phone us.

Early February 1992, saw the Health Minister herself setting out on a fact-finding tour across the province, presumably to test the birthing home waters. With a retinue of advisors in tow, Frances Lankin made guest appearances at several of the facilities already offering prenatal and postpartum services. She arrived at the St. Jacobs Family Birthing Home on February 13, 1992.

Calling St. Jacobs "an incredible model"[1] for others, Lankin went on to compliment the Home for its "energy and vision and community spirit," noting "it is taking community health care into its own hands and doing something about it."[2] Pressed by Board Members about their chances at being one of the three pilot centres selected, Lankin would not comment, but offered that "the community is well-positioned to submit a proposal."[3]

---

[1] "Health Minister Applauds Woolwich Facility as Model for Other Ontario Communities," *The Independent*, Elmira, February 24, 1992, p. 19.

[2] Ibid.

[3] Ibid.

Lankin saved special commendation for its primary midwife, Elsie Cressman. "I would like to say thank you, on behalf of women in Ontario."

Given the tortoise-like pace by which government usually moves, the next step in the Birthing Centre process came quickly, only six months after Lankin's tour of the province. On March 30, 1993 the government announced that it would now be hearing "Calls for Proposals" from any community group wishing to be considered as one of selected pilot Free-Standing Birthing Centres (FSBC's). This highly-anticipated announcement was followed by an invitation to interested groups and organizations to attend a series of meetings in Toronto. There applicants would be introduced to the method by which the applications would be made.

A comment in the March, 1993 issue of the St. Jacobs newsletter, *Update* only hints at the challenges that their proposal team would face in the application process:

> We had been hoping for it. We had been waiting for it. It was here at last. We contacted the Ministry of Health right away and received the Request from Proposals. One centimeter (73 pages) of paper. Twelve pages of preamble; six pages of instructions; scores of pages to be filled in – biographies, charts, fill-in-the-blanks; financial quotes; letters of support; budgets to be developed; staffing needs to be estimated, and on and on. It was overwhelming.

All submissions needed to be in in three months' time – June 30, 1993.

A team of four was assembled to tackle the proposal. Pat Legault, and Board Member Denise Squire would take on the lion's share job of drafting the weighty document. Denise had an MA from Wilfrid Laurier University in Community Psychology with a major in Midwifery. She had also logged many hours at the Birthing Home as a researcher.

The pair would be assisted by Board Members Brent Horst, who had expertise in financial matters and Judy McMullen. All work was volunteer, with no remuneration asked nor expected. With their strong community presence and support, and an unblemished history, the St. Jacobs group thought they had a good chance of being selected.

Over the next twelve weeks, much midnight oil was burned as the proposal writing team compiled the massive and all-encompassing document.[1] It included the group's mission statement and their proposal for services to be provided. Integral to the application were letters of support from influential community resources, flow charts, graphs, outlines and estimates of every conceivable facet of running a birthing home, from photocopy paper to the services of a lactation consultant.

The proposal also included a section on the impact that a free-standing birthing home would have on the geographical area and especially on the large number of Mennonite clients who would use the services.

The selected architect, The Walter Fedy Partnership of Kitchener estimated a figure of approximately $692,940.63 to design and build a fully-operational facility.[2] Staff salaries, including Administrator and Secretary, (not including midwives who would be funded from a different allocation) was a modest $42,000.[3]

As school let out for the summer, June 30, 1993, the St. Jacobs proposal was complete, and was delivered in person to the Ministry of Health Offices in Toronto. All that could be done to fulfill a decade-long dream was finished. Now all the birthing home could do was sit and wait. There was plenty going on, both at the Home and in the community to keep the midwives, staff and the Board of Directors busy.

[1] All references to the St. Jacobs bid to be selected as one of the Free-Standing Birthing Centres are drawn from interview with co-author Denise Squire, (now) Executive Director of the Woolwich Community Health Centre, June 2009.

[2] This compared to the modest Sudbury figure of only $210,000 and the "Cadillac" of the trio, the Toronto estimate of over $1,000,000.

[3] This compared to Sudbury's $97,000 and Toronto's $154,000.

Chapter Forty-Seven
Learning and More Learning

Elsie had little to do with the proposal. She gladly left that up to the St. Jacobs team.

> I didn't pay a lot of attention to all the facts and figures and really didn't know a lot of what was going on in that way. Pat and Denise knew what they were doing and that was all I had to know. Of course, I was still happy that it looked like we might have a chance to have a real Birthing Home, after all these years.

But as the clock ticked ever closer to the enactment of legislation, Elsie was walking on new ground of her own. She was becoming familiar with the Maternity Ward at the Kitchener-Waterloo Hospital, the main designated hospital for deliveries in the Waterloo Region. Wisely, knowing that midwives would be legally in hospitals soon, the Kitchener-Waterloo Hospital saw only positive outcomes from early "admission."

This was not the case for midwives in all Ontario communities. Andrea Horst puts the credit for Elsie's early entry to the hospital (in her official capacity) where she says it belongs—with Elsie herself. "Elsie's reputation was so strong, so good in the area that she was welcomed by most doctors and hospital administration. Elsie recalls it similarly:

> The nurses and doctors were good at K-W Hospital, and let me into the delivery room when one of my clients who wanted a hospital birth was due. I still couldn't legally deliver, but I could be there to "help." Before, if I was there at all, it was only to observe.

She vividly recalls two separate doctor incidents during this time:

> The OB, Dr. Halmo was late and the baby started to come. What was I supposed to do? Just stand there? So I gently and slowly began easing the baby out. Then Halmo arrived at the door with a nurse and everything stopped for a bit to see what would happen now. Now some doctors might have moved right in to take over when they saw what was happening, but he just stood there at the doorway watching me until it was over. After the baby was delivered, he came over and said to me: "Good job, Elsie."

Not all physicians were quite as hands-off as Dr. Halmo. A similar circumstance, at a different time, was underway with another absent doctor.

> The mother was having some problems delivering, not that they couldn't be solved by taking the birth slow and easy. That's the way we midwives did things. Most doctors though were all "let's get it done and over, fast."
>
> Well there I was doing it my way when the doctor suddenly arrived in the room. He saw me, walked to the bed, and reached right over my shoulder to administer the episiotomy. It was as if I wasn't even there. I had no legal right to even be there, so I could say nothing. But he knew I was mad. The baby was born quick after the episiotomy. He turned around to leave as soon as the baby came out and said to me "You can suture her." Which I did.

Elsie's fame had drawn healthy numbers of new clients to the St. Jacobs Family Birthing Home, so much so that by September 1993, there were four midwives in addition to Elsie practicing there. This large number becomes more impressive considering that midwifery was still paid for privately by the clients. Legislation was still some months away.

Chapter Forty-Eight
Old Midwives go Back to School

The year 1993, the final year before the Regulated Health Professionals Act was enacted, was a significant one for long-practicing midwives like Elsie Cressman. The regulatory Interim Regulatory Council on Midwifery (IRCM) of which St. Jacobs Board of Directors Chair Pat Legault was a member, had determined that these women would need to "establish competencies" before they were licensed to work legally in the province of Ontario.

Finding agreement on the best way to assess long-practicing midwives, like Elsie, in the business now for over forty years, took some concerted attention. Finally it was agreed to initiate a one-time assessment of skills. Proving competency in this examination would "grandmother" them into membership into the College of Midwives of Ontario.

Some midwives chafed at the assessment, but were assured that with the rules and regulations by which they now must adhere as legislated members of the health care system, came protection for them too.

Midwives were expected to enroll in a three-month term of study and assessment at the Michener Institute of Applied Health Sciences in Toronto. Always up for a new experience, Elsie looked forward to this opportunity. Her last time in school, in London, England had not been a positive one, academic or otherwise. But Midwife School in Canada would be fun! This old midwife was up for the challenge!

For the twelve-week period, Elsie took up residence in a dormitory close to the Michener campus. She settled in for learning, sharing and fellowship, and fondly recalls the experience:

> Some of the other "old" midwives said that there was too much work or that it was hard. But I didn't find it that way at all. In fact I enjoyed my time at Michener very much. We did work hard for sure, but I also had time to relax

and enjoy myself. And I learned a few things too.

The first and only graduates from the Midwifery "Grandmother's" Certification class of '93 attended ceremonies at the CN Tower to celebrate their success. Elsie reported the goings-on, with her usual good humour:

> We had caps and gowns and as I was walking up the steps to receive my diploma, if I didn't catch my gown with my foot and I almost fell. Thanks goodness I recovered and didn't embarrass myself by landing on the floor. I'm not sure if it was that, or that I was the oldest person on the graduation class, but I was the only one to get a kiss from the woman who was handing out the diplomas.

Elsie Cressman officially graduated from Michener Institute of Health Sciences Midwifery program on October 2, 1993. She was seventy years of age.

Chapter Forty-Nine
History and Honours

History may point to the passage of Bill 56, The Midwifery Act, part of the Regulated Health Professions Act as the New Democratic Party's greatest achievement in its brief tenure.[1] Yet, the political wheels of the legalization of midwifery had been rolling downhill for over ten years before the Rae government took power in October 1990.

Critics will look back too at the inordinate length of time between when the Bill was read into law on May 29, 1991, and when it was finally enacted, just over thirty-one months later, on January 1, 1994. Political debate aside, the Bill's passage was a milestone in the social fabric of Ontario. It set about to bring an era of uniformity to health in this province, proudly the first in Canada to recognize regulate and fund midwifery.

As legislated in the Midwifery Act, and detailed in the regulations of the governing College of Midwives of Ontario, midwives now provided, advocated, and practiced under the following tenets:[1]

- Continuity of Care
- Informed Choice
- Practice Sites and Choice of Birth Sites
- Regulations and Standard of Practice
- Policies and Guidelines
- Two Midwives at each Birth
- Midwife Practice at Hospital
- Community Input
- Liability Insurance
- Midwife Education and Continuing Education

[1] "The Midwifery Model of Practice in Ontario," The College of Midwives of Ontario, Revised 1994. The entire Midwifery Model of Practice may be viewed on-line at www.cmo.on.ca/downloads/H-MOP.pdf.

As if the enactment of midwifery legislation was not cause enough for Elsie Cressman to feel satisfaction and joy, some weeks into the New Year, her phone rang to tell her of another reason to celebrate.

She recalls an early morning telephone call she took in March of 1994:

> I was still in bed when the phone rang. It was someone from Toronto saying that I had been nominated for the Order of Ontario. I really hadn't even heard of this before, but I soon figured out it was pretty important. I was told to expect a formal invitation soon.

The prestigious Order of Ontario is the province's highest honour. It recognizes an outstanding contribution that Ontarians have made to their province and beyond, in the field of citizenship, public service, sports, the arts and health. Each year up to twenty-five Ontarians are invested into the Order, which allows its recipients to add O. Ont. after their surname.

Elsie and a friend, Jean Cober arrived in Toronto the evening before the investiture ceremony, and they were accommodated in a hotel. The glittering ceremony was held at the Ontario Legislature, the next day. There each of the twenty-five appointees was presented with a gold medal and a lapel pin in the form of Ontario's official flower, the Trillium. On the back of the pin their name had been engraved. Ontario's Lieutenant Governor Henry (Hal) Jackman presented the individual awards,

Afterwards all members then gathered for a group portrait. Other recipients invested at the same ceremony as Elsie included writer Alice Munro, the Honourable Flora MacDonald and businessman Ed Mirvish.

Elsie looks back on her investiture into the Order of Ontario as a great honour, but with characteristic understatement, she laughs: "I guess it was a big deal!" Still, the photo taken of all appointees hangs in the living room of her home. While Elsie's nominator was never revealed, she believes it was a former midwife client.

The sun was surely brightly shining on Elsie Cressman and the St. Jacobs Family Birthing Home, as winter melted into spring of 1994. The thaw would bring more sunshine to the little town, just north of Waterloo.

Chapter Fifty
Trailblazing Again

Elsie's honours continued well into 1994. She was unanimously selected to become "Head Midwife" at the Kitchener-Waterloo (K-W) Hospital.[1] Andrea Horst comments on this honour:

> There was no competition for the position. Hospital officials decided unanimously that it would be Elsie. Who else was better known or respected in the community than Elsie Cressman? So who else could it have been?

This honour was a coup for Elsie, now seventy-one years of age. But it came with considerable responsibilities too. With no systems in place to envelop midwives into the hospital community, formalities and rules needed to be conceived and implemented. Midwives who had completed the Michener training, and new midwives out of university would need to apply to be allowed hospital privileges. A Medical Advisory Board on which Elsie sat would consider these applications.

It was largely due to Elsie that these procedures were implemented smoothly and seamlessly. Andrea Horst states, with assurance:

> Moving the midwives into hospitals across Ontario didn't come without some problems, more in some hospitals than others. But at Grand River things went smoothly. And that was due to Elsie more than anyone.

Denise Squire, now Executive Director of the Woolwich Community Health Centre in St. Jacobs pays equal complement to Elsie for her early midwifery hospital work:

> Elsie had to navigate her way through uncharted waters, through the maze of GPs, Obstetricians, Heads of Staff

[1] Elsie continued on in this role at the Kitchener-Waterloo Hospital (renamed Grand River Hospital in 1995) until her retirement in 1998.

> and Hospital Administration. And she did it admirably. Her early work made the transition so much smoother for the midwives who came after her. They should have, and most did, give Elsie a big vote to thanks for the work she did for them.

Longtime supporter Pat Legault also praises Elsie's early work in the hospital:

> She was very respected right across the medical community, and this helped smooth the integration of the midwives into Grand River Hospital. But she was also smart and astute. She knew that she couldn't alienate the medical establishment by making demands or being pushy. She didn't, and she wasn't, and it paid off for everybody.

Amazement might have been felt by some, who had worked with Elsie at Shirati Medical Mission more than twenty years earlier, to see her in such a position of authority. At Shirati, in her role as protector and advisor to leprosy patients, Elsie had been a self-acclaimed stone in the shoe of authorities, both missionary and African. Like a bulldog with a meaty bone, she'd determinedly sought better care for her patients in the face of continuing prejudice against their condition.

During Africa's nationalistic period of the early 1970's when institutions had sought to replace "European" authority figures with Africans, Elsie had been replaced. But she'd had another strike against her as well, one that had virtually guaranteed her removal.

From his home in Pennsylvania, former Eastern Mennonite Board of Missions administrator Hershey Leaman recalls that the same assertiveness which had gained improvements in patient care at her Leprosarium, had not won Elsie fans in the Shirati administration.

But Elsie had learned a thing or two about methods over the ensuing years. She'd ascertained to whom she could give a nudge in the Kitchener-Waterloo medical establishment; to whom she must give a wider berth. Elsie was no fool, and had learned to use diplomacy in her dealings with "higher-ups." And it got her everywhere! Had those in the upper echelon of Shirati Medical Mission been able to see the "later Elsie" in action, they must surely have had occasion to blink their eyes twice.

Elsie's honours brought further recognition to the St. Jacobs Family Birthing Home too, which grew in size and stature. "This was because of Elsie's reputation all over Ontario," Andrea Horst acknowledges. There was a downside to being popular though. Elsie had more clients than she could handle. Fortunately her "glamour factor" enticed a number of well-qualified new midwives to St. Jacobs, all wanting to work alongside her. "It was a feather in their cap to be associated with Elsie," says Andrea.

Elsie was also in demand as a speaker, and she made numerous presentations to both physicians' and nurses' groups. Her skills at turning breech babies or External Cephalic Version (ECV) was especially prized, and she was often invited to share her expertise in this specialized area. From time to time, "enlightened" physicians sent patients to her for breech turning.

Little could Elsie have foreseen how this gift would one day turn her world upside down.

Chapter Fifty-One
The Birthing Centre Debacle

Some weeks after the Call for Proposals deadline, it was announced that a total of twelve applications from various organizations across the province had been received. An agonizing ten-month wait period now ensued.

And the wheels of government ground slowly forward. It became clear to all that Health Minister Lankin's wish to have designated Free-Standing Birthing Centres up and running by the time legislation was enacted was a pipe dream existing only in the Minister's ambitious mind.

Indeed, by the time notification of the selections had been made, eighteen months after the London announcement, Lankin had moved out of the Health portfolio into the high profile Ministry for Economic Development and Trade. She was replaced by Ruth Grier, to whom fell the happy task of announcing the selections, in April 1994.

To the surprise of no one at the St. Jacobs Family Birthing Home, it was announced that St. Jacobs would join Sudbury and Toronto as one of the three pilot Free-Standing Birthing Centres. The community of Fort Albany on James Bay, which would serve largely a native population, would become a surprise fourth site.

Terms of the package would be forthcoming from the Ministry. It was understood, however, that the government would cover all operating costs of the Birthing Centres, as well as any renovations to existing buildings. The cost of the "shell" would be the responsibility of each centre itself.[1]

With these details now in place, the St. Jacobs Board wasted no time in securing property. On August 25, 1994, their Board of Directors closed a deal that saw them purchase a parcel of property and a house at 9 Parkside Drive, a stone's throw from the Woolwich Community

[1] Interview Denise Squire, June 2009.

Health Centre. The $40,000 cost was covered by money raised from donations and various fundraising initiatives.

Over the fall of 1994 and the winter of 1995, the group sought input as to the future of the parcel. After weighing several alternatives, it was decided that the cost to renovate the existing house would be ill-spent. They would build a new structure. A local resident bought the house – a bargain at $5000 – and moved it to a new location. The job of designing the new Centre now moved into full swing.

But had a crystal ball been consulted during this joyous time, a dark figure might have been spotted lurking on the horizon. His name? Mike Harris.

Chapter Fifty-Two
The "Common-Sense" Revolution

As Ontarians went to the polls in October 1995, the province was mired in a record deficit. Many blamed it on the runaway spending of the province's first socialist-leaning government, the New Democratic Party.

Progressive Conservative leader Mike Harris and his "Common Sense Revolution" struck a chord with Ontarian's pocketbooks and his party swept to power, winning 82 seats to the NDP's 17. Ontario's first flirtation with the New–Age Socialism had ended in the voter's booths.

Harris wasted no time in getting "Common Sense" off the ground. One of his government's first announcements was the closing of the provinces Free-Standing Birthing Centres. Harris called them "a duplication of services."

Political and media reaction to the cancellation of the FSBC's was mixed. The October 6, 1995 Kitchener Record editorial entitled "Death of Birth Centres is Sad but Inevitable," clearly sided with the government. "No matter how one cuts it, birthing centres would duplicate services already available elsewhere. And they would have benefited only a few communities,"[1] Sudbury MPP Floyd Laugren, Finance Critic in the former NDP government predictably bemoaned the cancellation, accusing the Conservatives of "using economics as an excuse to implement right wing philosophies."[2]

In St. Jacobs, Denise Squire vividly recalls the announcement of the cancellation:

> I was driving in my car and Jim Wilson, the new Progressive Conservative Health Minister came on the

[1] Editorial, "Death of Birthing Centres is Sad but Inevitable," *The Kitchener-Waterloo Record*, Friday, October 6, 1995.

[2] Richard Brenner, "Dropping Birth Units Targets Women, Critic says," *The Kitchener-Waterloo Record*, October 7 1995.

news to announce that the funding had been withdrawn for the Birthing Centres. I was stunned; I couldn't quite believe my ears, and remember saying to myself: "It's over; it's over."

Her shock must have been greater, given that barely three weeks before, she and Pat Legault had met with Health Minister Wilson to explore how the Birthing Centre process could be speeded up. Wilson gave no indication in that meeting of the impending doom. "We heard it on the radio and read it in the paper like everyone else."

The final blow for the future of FSBCs in Ontario was not just the withdrawal of funds for the four chosen sites, but the decree that such facilities would not be allowed to exist in Ontario at all. As the agreement between the previous NDP government and the centres had been "on promise," and no legislation had ever been passed to enact their creation, dissolution was done effortlessly.

The official response to the announcement from the St. Jacobs Family Birthing Home came in the December 1995 issue of *The Update*. Its muted tone belies what must have been the devastation felt by all. "We are deeply saddened by the short-sighted decision of the Ministry of Health to limit availability of cost-effective birthing options for the women and children of Ontario."

Denise Squire details what was left for the St. Jacobs Family Birthing Home to accomplish after the "Common Sense" bulldozer made history of their well-laid out plans.

> At the time of the announcement we were literally ready to start the equipment digging in the ground. Now everything needed to be closed down. In the short term, we had bills to pay. We'd taken out a loan at the bank for the preparatory work on the site. Our thinking of course was that would come back to us in the start-up package we had been told was forthcoming from the government.

She adds that to give the Harris government its dues, neither they nor the other pilot FSBHs were left hanging financially. "Everyone who was owed money was paid in full." In the long term however, the

Board had another "sticky wicket." They now owned a piece of prime real estate property, purchased largely from donations given them by the public. "And we had no hope at least in the foreseeable future to be able to do anything with it," says Denise. Ontario laws stated that they would have five years in which to disperse these assets.

Discussion carried on for almost four years about the property's fate. Finally in 1999, after considerable debate and consideration, the property was transferred to the St. Jacobs Birthing Home's good friend and neighbour, the Woolwich Community Health Centre. "There'd been such a bond between the two groups for many years," Denise says, "that it seemed the perfect union."

When Denise later became Executive Director of the Woolwich Family Health Centre, this sealed the symbiotic relationship between the two St. Jacobs neighbours. "It gave our community what it needed and deserved; and that was a complete range of health care," she says.

Chapter Fifty-Three
Permanently Settled

In recompense for the land, the Woolwich Community Health Centre agreed to build the Midwives a permanent facility which the group would rent at a reasonable rate. Having had more addresses, over their decade-long history, than a Waterloo County apple tree has apples, the midwives were settled for good.

It was understood also in the agreement, that extra rooms would be constructed, in the event free-standing birthing homes again came on the political radar. In the meantime, the space would be leased to other medical groups: naturopaths, chiropractors or physiotherapists.

On January 2, 2002, the St. Jacobs Family Birthing Home Practice took up their present location at 9 Parkside Drive, within a stone's throw from their landlord, the Woolwich Community Health Centre. They were pleased with their surroundings which included four examining rooms, several offices, a large airy waiting room and a staff room. The liaison was strengthened when, that same year, the Ministry of Health approved the Woolwich Community Health Centre as the Transfer Agent through which all expenses at the birthing home, including the midwives salaries would be paid.[1]

The Midwives' Board of Directors had continued to meet sporadically, but inevitably, they realized that their goals had been met. They now lacked a purpose. It seemed an opportune time to close their books. With their dissolution, the St. Jacobs Family Birthing Home Inc. officially became the St. Jacobs Midwives.

Brent Horst, a member of the Board since 1984 looks back at their long and occasionally bumpy journey.

> We'd been together for over ten years and had accomplished so much. This included being one of only

[1] Midwife Clinics in Ontario are not funded directly through the Ministry of Health but have funds funneled through (usually) partnering medical clinics in the community.

> four locations in the whole of Ontario to be selected to have a free-standing birthing home. What an amazing accomplishment! Then, when things went the way they did after the 1995 election, it was such a heart-break to all of us.

Brent pays tribute to Elsie Cressman as the inspiration and push behind their lofty goals:

> None of it would ever have gotten off the ground had it not been for Elsie, though. It was because of her that we started and it was through Elsie that we got where we were. She was the reason St. Jacobs Midwives became what they did.

Elsie puts her own perspective on the events that grabbed deadlines for herself, her colleagues, her practice and the little town of St. Jacobs, from 1981 to 1995.

> The idea of a birthing home was wonderful idea, but its time just hadn't come. And maybe it wouldn't have been used by a lot of clients anyway. There's just something so nice about giving birth at home in a women's own bed.

Chapter Fifty-Four
Time to Say Goodbye

Still delivering babies at age seventy-five, Elsie had finally begun to feel her age. She'd cut back to part-time when her long-standing hip and back problems began limiting her activities and movement. In 1998, into her seventy-sixth year, she decided to retire. Her friends in St. Jacobs planned not just one retirement party for their inspiration and leader, but two.

The first, to take place on November 6, 1998 would be a farewell dinner attended by Elsie, as guest of honour, her friends and family, colleagues and Board of Directors at the St. Jacobs Family Birthing Home, and representative of the Woolwich Community Health Centre.

Two days later, the "Big Bash" would take place at Waterloo's large Rotary Centre. The space was needed, as the guest list was expected to be of "army" proportions. Invitations to the party had gone out to hundreds of Elsie's former clients, asking them to come to say goodbye to the woman who had delivered their babies into the world. The "Elsie-babies" were, of course, invited too.

A crowd of 500 was expected including almost 200 children. A special guest was Taylor Mellway, 18 of Ottawa. Taylor was the first baby Elsie had delivered in Ontario. A lasting memory for Elsie was a group portrait of herself and her babies – ranging in age from 11 weeks, the last baby Elsie delivered, to Taylor, almost an adult. Waterloo Progressive Conservative MPP Elizabeth Witmer, the Minister of Health was also guest, and she gave tribute to Ontario's "First Midwife."

St. Jacobs Practice Administrator Andrea Horst puts an insider's perspective on the contribution that Elsie Cressman made to her place of work, her community and her society – a contribution that remains intact today, more than a dozen years after Elsie's retirement:

> The St. Jacobs Midwives today still ride on Elsie's reputation. People know that this is where she practiced and we still continue to bear the good fortune of this. And our midwives are very aware of who she was, and what she meant to us. They are still in awe of her.

She talks too about Elsie's perception of her own charisma:

> Elsie liked having the reputation she had, and she did like the attention. And yes she was ambitious, but not for herself. Attention, ambition and power for Elsie was all about giving that power to women. The power for them to determine what they wanted with their pregnancy, and how their babies were born. And if she was the means by which this could happen and people paid attention to her for it, then that was OK too.

In a perfect world, Elsie Cressman would have rested on her esteemed laurels and eased into retirement. She might have done some traveling, visited with friends, cooked African meals for get-togethers and read "trashy" novels. But fate was to assault Elsie with a mighty blow within weeks of her retirement party.

Part Six

The Trial

Chapter Fifty-five
Baby Paul

On May 25, 1985, Christine Carere visited her midwife Elsie Cressman, at the St. Jacobs Family Birthing Home. While neither party anticipated it, the meeting would change both women's lives.[1]

This would be Christine's seventh baby and she hoped for a home birth. She'd contacted Elsie early into her pregnancy and over the next several months kept regular appointments with her. Her progress was uneventful, until her 30th week. Then during a routine examination, Elsie had discovered that Christine's baby was in the double-footling breech position. The head of the fetus was pointed up, and the two feet were pointing down. The baby was also lying in the posterior position, facing the mother's back.

Given these complications, Elsie could not agree to delivering Christine's baby at home. When her labour started, Christine would need to enter the hospital and have a Caesarian Section. But there was another option if Christine agreed. Elsie could attempt to turn the baby in a procedure known as External Cephalic Version (ECV). This procedure would see Elsie placing her hands on Christine's belly, and expertly massaging the fetus in a way that it would respond and turn right side up. Elsie had perfected the ECV over hundreds of breech babies and indeed had even demonstrated her skills to the medical establishment. If she was successful in turning the baby, then Christine's wishes to have a home birth could be actualized.

[1] All references to the trial of Midwife Elsie Cressman are based on the document: "Ontario Superior Court of Justice between Christene Carere and Paul Joseph Carere, by his litigation guardian Christine Carere, Rachelle Judith Carere, by her litigation guardian Christine Carere, and April Lynn Carere by her litigation guardian Christine Carere and Norah Ruth Carere Plaintiffs and Elsie Cressman, St. Jacobs Family Birthing Home Inc. Defendants."

But at seven months pregnancy, it was too early to attempt an ECV. In fact, the baby might still turn of its own accord. Elsie suggested that they wait a month and see what happened. That was agreeable to Christine.

The month passed and Christine arrived at the St. Jacobs Clinic for her next scheduled appointment with Elsie. She'd decided that if the baby was still in the footling/breech position, she'd be willing to have Elsie try to turn it during the visit. If indeed the baby hadn't moved of its own accord.

On examination, Elsie confirmed that the baby remained in the same position. With directions from Christine, Elsie began the procedure. Her first step would be to attempt to massage the fetus from its posterior position. If that was unsuccessful then the ECV to turn it from breech could not proceed.

For the next ten minutes, Elsie expertly massaged, moving her hands to various positions. Feeling the urge to void, Christine excused herself and left for the bathroom. When she returned, telling Elsie that indeed she had had a bowel movement, Elsie noted that this might be a sign of early labour. The massaging procedure then continued. After several minutes, with no success, Elsie decided to discontinue her work for another visit. The appointment ended, and the Carere's left for home.

On the way, Christine was alarmed to realize that she was bleeding from her vagina. She alerted her husband Fred, the driver, to return to the Birthing Home. While Christine remained in the car, Fred ran inside to alert Elsie, who immediately left what she was doing to rush to the Carere vehicle. Alarmed at her client's condition she ordered Fred to take his wife to the Kitchener-Waterloo Hospital immediately.

Christine was admitted to the hospital, at 7:50 PM, and was placed in Obstetrics under the supervision of Dr. O'Brien. She did not inform hospital staff about the ECV attempt. Over the course of the next four hours, she continued to bleed. At some point she asked Dr. O'Brien if she should have an ultrasound. The doctor rejected this, saying that it was hospital policy not to move women out of Obstetrics for tests. Approximately one hour later, Christine informed Dr. O'Brien of the attempted ECV. His response was to "wait and see."

When midnight came, with no cessation of bleeding, a decision was made to deliver the baby by Caesarean Section and Christine was taken to the operating room. Shortly thereafter, she gave birth to a son. The baby, named Paul was approximately six weeks premature and suffering from Respiratory Distress Syndrome, hypovolemic shock and anemia. Hospital staff ventilated and intubated the wee one and he was transferred two days later to McMaster University Medical Centre.

The health problems for baby Paul Carere were only beginning. He had gait problems, due to spasticity in his lower limbs, and didn't walk until he was over two years of age. At age three, he was diagnosed with Cerebral Palsy. There were intellectual delays as well. He entered a modified program at school and needed assistance to complete language and arithmetic assignments. In his early teenage years, he functioned academically at the level of a Grade 2 student. Throughout his childhood Paul was monitored at the Rotary Centre and received support from the Centre's Orthopedic Specialists.

Yet it was not until 1999, when Paul was fourteen that Christine Carere began to question if the circumstances of Paul's birth had precipitated his physical and intellectual problems. After discussion and consultation with several professionals, she decided to take legal action against the midwife who had cared for her – Elsie Cressman. On the 19th of January 1999, Elsie was served with papers telling her that "A Legal Proceeding has been commenced against you by the Plaintiffs." The plaintiffs named were Christine Carere and her son Paul, as well as the three Carere daughters: Rachelle, April and Nora.

Elsie recalls her reaction on first seeing the papers.

> It surprised me of course, but in the back of my mind I always knew that something like this might happen. I had full confidence that what I was doing was safe, but

> something could happen at any time. Of all the hundreds of babies that I'd turned successfully, this was one that hadn't gone as planned.

Four full years would pass before the trial actually took place. This time allowed the lawyers to prepare and build their cases, contact their witnesses and read all pertinent documents. Jim Sloan, one of the two Prosecuting Attorneys for the case, the other being Peter Madorin, was thankful for the time.

> My learning curve for this case was steep. I needed to become familiar with midwifery and learn all the terminology. I'd certainly never heard words like External Cephalic Version, Grande Multiparous or Placenta Previa before, and I needed to know them and fully understand them before I could do my job.[1]

Representing Elsie for the Defense would be Toronto lawyer Deborah Berlach. Berlach had been retained by the Insurance Company for the Association of Ontario Midwives.

There were several charges[1] against Elsie that the court proceedings needed to decide.

> 1. Did the ECV procedure cause Paul's Cerebral Palsy?
> 2. Did Elsie Cressman perform the ECV in a negligent manner?
> 3. Did Elsie Cressman fail to inform Carere as to the nature and risks of the ECV prior to obtaining consent to perform the ECV?
> 4. If Elsie Cressman was negligent, did the negligence cause some or all of Paul's present condition?
> 5. If Paul's present condition was caused by the Negligence of Elsie Cressman, at what amount should the damages be assessed?

---

[1] Interview with (now) Justice James Sloan, Prosecuting Attorney for Carere vs. Cressman Trial. May 2009.

Chapter Fifty-Six
The Proceedings

The trial of Carere vs. Cressman began on January 7, 2002. It took place in a Kitchener Court House over sixteen days, concluding on February 1, 2002. Presiding Judge was Mr. Justice Henderson. Various witnesses for both the Defense and Prosecution were called to testify. The "star witness" for the Defense was Eileen Hutton, now the Assistant Dean of Midwifery at McMaster University. She was an expert in External Cephalic Version.[1]

For the Defense:

Hutton's written report[1] for the Defense is, in part noted here:

1. Timing of Procedure. As is evidenced in both reference texts and articles, ECV in the last trimester (after 28 weeks) was acceptable practice. Thus the ECV at between 33 and 34 weeks would be considered appropriate practice.

2. When the contraindications for ECV that were available in 1985 were reviewed, there is no reason to have excluded Mrs. Carere from having an ECV done. There was no evidence of pre-clampsia or hypertension, no prior uterine scar, no history of pre-term labour...

3. When undertaking the ECV for Mrs. Carere, Ms. Cressman was suspicious of her bowel movement and recognizing that this could be a sign of early labour, she stopped the procedure. The ECV procedure appears to have been undertaken according to the principles laid out in the literature. Ms. Cressman's understanding of the procedure and contraindications seem appropriate.

4. Informed Consent. Implicit consent was provided when Mrs. Carere presented herself at the Midwife Clinic to have her breech baby turned.

[1] Report Regarding the Care Provided by Elsie Cressman, prepared by Eileen Hutton, RM, MNSc

5. Attendance with Client to Hospital. When she presented with frank bleeding, Ms. Cressman immediately sent the Carere's to Kitchener–Waterloo Hospital but did not accompany them. This is a reflection of the unregulated status of midwives in 1985 and the reluctance of many hospitals to allow midwives into the hospital.

6. The Use of Ultrasounds. Midwives had no access to ultrasounds in 1985. And at that time and for several years to follow, there was debate in the literature regarding the relative safety of ultrasound.

For the Prosecution:

There were two main witnesses for the Prosecution. One was Dr. Steinburg, an Obstetrician. The other was British Midwife and university lecturer Muriel O'Driscoll.[1] Lawyer (now Judge) Jim Sloan explains why a British midwife was called to testify instead using a Canadian or American one:

> We could not find a North American midwife who would testify against Elsie Cressman. That is how well she was regarded in the midwifery community. We had to go across the ocean before we could find someone appropriate and who would be a credible resource.

O'Driscoll's testimony revolved around several key points that are outlined below:

1. Midwives should be aware of the high risks of a grande multiparous woman (women who have had five or more deliveries). Christine was a grande multiparous, having had six previous children.

2. A home birth would not be advised for such a grande multiparous woman, and information should be given to the client to enable her to make an informed choice. With a grande multiparous woman, due to the overstretched and overused uterus, there are risks of a low lying placenta.

3. On finding the fetus presenting by the breech at 33 ¾ weeks of pregnancy, the correct management would have been to refer Mrs. Carere for an ultrasound scan to determine gestation and fetal

[1] Report by Muriel O'Driscoll of Liverpool, U.K.

normality and to eliminate placenta previa (placenta has pulled away from the uterine wall exposing the raw surface of the placenta.)

4. Turning the breech by External Cephalic Version can be a hazardous undertaking. No midwife should undertake this procedure, unless there is no other way that a woman can get an obstetric opinion.

5. In this case, where there appeared to be resistance and pain, more than one attempt was made. No midwife should act this way.

6. On the return of Mrs. Carere to the midwife, following the procedure, she was bleeding vaginally. This is a deviation from the normal and at this time the midwife should have either called for an emergency paramedic or an obstetrician.

Chapter Fifty-Seven
Elsie Takes the Stand

Elsie took the stand in her own defense. Then Counsel Jim Sloan recalls Elsie as a confident witness.

> Elsie came across as a "take charge" kind of person, and I say that in a good way. It was readily apparent how much knowledge she had. And the Carere situation on May 25, 1985 had been a "take charge" kind of moment for Elsie. "This baby is in breech and I can fix it."

The following is an excerpt of cross-examination on the stand, between Elsie and Prosecutor Jim Sloan. Sloan was questioning Elsie on the details of the conversation which took place between herself and Christine prior to the ECV attempt.

> Q: (by Counsel Sloan) There's some discussion that there was in fact a placenta previa before you started the external version. Did you do anything to ascertain whether or not there was a placenta previa?
>
> A: No I did not.
>
> Q: Prior to doing it, did you discuss with Mrs. Carere that if there was a placenta previa there may be problems in doing an external version?
>
> A: I don't think that I did, because I expect my clients to be well-versed. At that time when we did midwifery, it was outside of the medical profession. Both the client and I were doing something that was not thought of well by the medical profession, which is understandable. Therefore I expect my clients who came and sought me out to avail themselves of anything they could do to get information on birth ... I urged my clients to be knowledgeable about birth ...

> And the first thing, the first complication of pregnancy is – that you would read about, I'm sure, – uh is breeches and placenta previa. It's something that happens once in every 2000 births or so. I just forget right now but it's a very rare thing. So I am not sure if I mentioned it at all.

A sticking point between Elsie and the Prosecution was the issue of the patient's pain during the procedure. Elsie denies ever hearing Christine say that she was in pain. "If she had said there was pain, I would have stopped, but she never did," Elsie states.

Mr. Justice Henderson's report was released on April 16. Its findings were in favour of the plaintiff, Christine Carere. In part, they follow:

> I find that Cressman negligently failed to properly inform Carere of the nature of the ECV, and that a reasonable patient in Carere's particular position who had been properly informed, would not have consented to the ECV. She was not made aware of the risks of placental abruption, cord entanglement, hemorrhage, uterine rupture, ruptured membranes, fetal distress premature labour, fetal demise or maternal death.
>
> In response to the question: "did negligence cause the plaintiff's damages?" the answer should be obvious. If Cressman was negligent because she performed the ECV in a high-risk situation, then it follows that the ECV should not have been performed at all. Further, if Cressman was negligent because she performed the ECV without first locating the placenta, then it follows the ECV should never have been performed because the location of the placenta in this case would have been an absolute contra-indication to performing the ECV.

The damages to the Carere family were substantial.

General damages of Paul:	$225,000
Future loss of income of Paul:	$949,000
Future care costs of Paul:	$2,059,977
FLA claim of Carere and her daughters:	$217,694
For a total of:	$3,651,691

This claim would be paid by the Encon Insurance Managers Insurance Company on behalf of the Association of Ontario Midwives.

In an interview given to Kitchener Record writer Brian Caldwell after the settlement was announced, Elsie was philosophical: "You take the bitter with the sweet. I've had so much gratitude that I guess I can take one bad thing." She continues, "In hindsight I don't think I could have done anything differently."

Seven years after the suit she says:

> I'll admit that the attempt to turn caused the bleeding. I wish I could have predicted it. I had never had a woman with a placenta previa before. I don't think I had ever put my hands on a placenta previa tummy.

Elsie continues to dispute Christine's claim of expressing pain to her during the procedure. "She never said that to me." She also finds fault with Christine being allowed to bleed for five hours in K-W Hospital before action was taken to deliver her baby.

Given that her retirement had started only two months before she was served the papers of the legal action, Elsie had been unable to move on with her life. Now she could. As before, during troubled days in her life, her faith in God sustained her. "And I always have to try to love that woman (Christine Carere)," she states firmly.

Part Seven

Retirement, finally

Chapter Fifty-Eight
Losing a Cherished Independence

In 2004, Elsie made the decision to sell her Driftwood Avenue house in Kitchener and move into a retirement home. After years of pain and restricted movement, she'd had hip replacement surgery, and while the surgery was a success, Elsie found the upkeep of a house more than she could handle. She told her nephew Brian of her decision to downsize and he took over, putting his aunt's house on the market privately. It quickly sold.

She then moved to Nithview Retirement Home in New Hamburg, in one of the assisted-living apartments. Her foster sister, Lillian Bean and Lillian's husband Gordon came to Nithview to live around the same time. Elsie's surroundings suited her well. With no maintenance tasks to burden her, she was free to spend her time as she liked. At age 81 she was still driving her own vehicle and was able to indulge in two of her favourite activities – shopping and socializing. Before long, she and Lillian had discovered a pleasant way to while away the hours – completing challenging jig-saw puzzles.

At age 83, she grudgingly gave up her car, on the insistence of her nieces and nephews. "It was so hard to do, and took away so much of my independence," she says. The independent woman with the "go-go" lifestyle was now restricted as to whom she saw and where she went. One of her greatest losses was dropping by the farm after church to visit with her sister-in-law Gladys Cressman.

A woman who had found it easy to make friends in her youth and middle age, she found finding soul mates more difficult as a senior. Now time hung heavily on her shoulders.

Elsie's prospects improved when she got a motorized scooter. In good weather she could wend her way to downtown New Hamburg or to the nearby MCC Thrift Store, but this was still a poor substitute for real independence.

Afternoon tea time, crokinole games and puzzle time with Lillian filled time too. Sunday was reserved for church. She greatly looked forward to Pastor Earl Koch's sermons and the fellowship she found at Grace Mennonite Church.

And so the days melted into weeks, months and years. The winter of 2008 unexpectedly offered her a respite from what she frankly calls her "boring life."

Kitchener residents Karen Stainton and her husband Bruce Payne were fond of Elsie, who had been the midwife for the couple's two children. They'd learned some details of the road she'd travelled through life and found them compelling. "We felt that Elsie's story was worth telling," Karen Stainton explains, "especially the African period."[1]

They were fans too of the documentary film work done by Kitchener-Waterloo residents Paul and Paula Campsall of Meta Media Production Company and wondered if Meta Media might be interested in talking to Elsie with a view to documenting her life. The Campsalls were immediately taken with Elsie. Paula Campsall recalls:

> What made the story even more attractive to us was the vast amount of support material that Elsie had. She had hundreds of slides and audiotapes that she had recorded to send home to friends and family in Canada during her Africa days.[2]

It soon became apparent to both the Campsalls and the Payne-Staintons how important Elsie's African days were in her life, and how dearly she wished to return. Before long, documenting Elsie's story had added a new chapter. They envisioned Elsie returning to Africa for a visit, and that journey being recorded. "It was just a question of finding the money to send her there," Karen Stainton says. "We decided that Bruce and I would be the primary fundraisers for this

[1] Interview with Karen Stainton and Bruce Payne, July 2009.

[2] Interview Paula Campsall, July 2009.

venture and the Campsalls would look after the logistics of the trip. The neophyte fundraisers were treading new waters in this initiative, but were keen to begin. They learned their ABC's quickly.

"It quickly became apparent that without status as a charitable organization we would not be getting very far," Bruce Payne states. A glimmer of light shone in the venture when the Campsalls, who had strong connections with CTV producer-director Paul Francescutti approached him about the network's possible interest in the story. On the strength of that connection, and the promise that the documentary would be offered to CTV exclusively, the Campsells were granted $5000 "seed money," to get the project up and running.

Meanwhile, the Payne-Staintons continued to beat the community bushes for money. An event in Elsie's honour was held in September 2008 at the Wilmot Recreation Centre. There Elsie friends and supporters were made aware of the Africa project and donations were accepted to cover the costs of the journey. This event raised some financial support but not nearly enough to book airline tickets to Africa.

The Campsalls had also made application to the Canadian Economic Development Agency (CEDA) for financial support. Having had experience applying to this federal funding agency before, and knowing the type of projects CEDA looked on favourably, the Campsalls knew the correct way to ask for money. They key was to partner with other humanitarian agencies in making their request for funds. As such they made connections with Caring Partners, a medical clinic at Matangwe, Kenya; Eastern Mennonite Missions who continue to support Shirati Hospital; a World Vision Clinic in Voi, Kenya and the Mission Aviation Fellowship (MAF) which offers humanitarian, relief and development organization through aviation. All agencies had strong Canadian connections.

The Campsalls proposed to CEDA that in addition to filming Elsie as she went about on her African reunion, they would film and interview Canadians working at these partner agencies. A stop was also proposed at the Tom Mboya Health Centre on Rusinga Island, Kenya where Elsie had worked for three years.

Paula Campsall offers another reason why CEDA looked favourably on the Meta Media application. "That we had done a fair bit of fundraising before we applied to CEDA was an important factor in us getting the grant." She notes that the Meta Media application was granted unanimously by the CEDA decision-makers.

Chapter Fifty-Nine
Return to Africa

A group of five individuals left Canada on November 26, 2009 for their fourteen-day African adventure. Paula Campsall would be acting in her role as producer of the venture and Paul Campsall would fill the role as editor and director. They would be joined by Paul Francescutti, as film operator. Elsie and her private duty Nurse Barbie Butts who had volunteer experience with charitable organizations overseas would fill seats four and five on the plane. Elsie would get around in a rented wheelchair and walker.

Flying KLM to Amsterdam, the group continued on to Nairobi, Kenya. Then it was on to the Matangwe Health Clinic, run by Kenyan natives and former Kitchener-Waterloo residents Stephen and Sylvia Scott. Their clinic provides primary diagnostic and emergency care to Africans in need of medical attention. The area is a "hotspot" for AIDS, malaria, tuberculosis and typhoid infection and transmission. There Elsie reunited with her niece Evelyn, a midwife who was presently doing volunteer work at the Scott's Clinic. It was during this stop where Elsie's long-dormant familiarity with the Swahili language was revived. She conversed easily in a language she had not used regularly for over thirty years. "I guess it just never left me," Elsie laughs.

Then it was on to Rusinga Island, where Elsie had managed the Tom Mboya Health Clinic between 1971 and 1975. Changes were a-plenty, since she'd last stepped foot on the scenic island. Residents and visitors no longer had to rely on the ferry to come and go to the mainland. A causeway now links the island to the mainland. Elsie was filmed there meeting Father Tilan, a Catholic priest whom she knew during her time on Rusinga. The interviewer is heard to ask Father Tilan: "did Elsie do good work when she was on Rusinga?" Father Tilan responds: "She didn't do good work, she did excellent work."

Once an idyllic destination away from the hustle and bustle of the Kenya mainland, Rusinga is now a bee-hive of activity. "I couldn't believe the number of cars on the island," Elsie observed, recalling a time when the only method of transportation was on foot or bicycle. The pace of the Mboya clinic gave her another surprise. "The three of us were run off our feet when I was there. Now with more staff, they seem to have time on their hands."

The bustling Shirati Hospital was the group's next stop. There a breakfast was held in Elsie's honour, and many of her former leprosy patients attended. "They all knew me, but there were very few I remembered well," Elsie recalls. She was touched by the number of testimonials she heard. A reunion with her former ward Jerosa, now a grandmother of four, was a highlight of the Shirati visit.

Elsie was astounded to see the number of new buildings on the hospital site. "I could hardly even find my old nurses' residence," she comments. She travelled to the old Leprosarium site, which is now derelict. The condition of the buildings saddened her. "They'd even taken the cement benches out of the Assembly Hall."

While Meta Media continued filming at the World Vision organization in Voi Kenya, then carried on to interview Guelph native, pilot Daniel Loewen-Rudgers of Mission Aviation Fellowship, Elsie and Barbie took in the sights of the Maasai Mara Game Reserve in Kenya. There they were housed in deluxe tents, complete with washroom facilities. During one meal in the camp dining room, she and Barbie were startled when a group of kitchen workers came out to the eating area banging pots and pans and blowing horns. "They were carrying a birthday cake which they presented to one of the tourists," Elsie says. The next day the same procession came out and headed her way. They were carrying another cake and placed it in front of her. A message in Swahili was inscribed. Elsie translated for the non-Swahili speakers. "It said Goodbye; Come Again."

The four "junior" members of the party were amazed at the 86-year old Elsie's stamina and appetite for activity. "She wanted to do everything and was usually the first one up in the morning to get going," Paula Campsall chuckles. Elsie herself thanks the other members of the group for getting her wheelchair in and out of vehicles. "I was carried around like royalty," she laughs.

In the blink of an eye, Elsie's return journey to Africa was at an end. She had very mixed feelings about her return home. "It would be nice to sleep in my own bed again," she admits, "but it would not be easy to move from the 'go-go-go' of the trip, to the boredom of being at home."

The fatigue of fourteen days of travel only presented itself after her return.

Elsie's return to Africa was a fitting tribute to a woman who played many roles in her long life – nurse, missionary, midwife, adventurer, "big game" hunter, teacher, pastor, counselor, advocate and foster mother. She reflects on the experience:

> My family at home hadn't wanted me to go on the trip. They thought it would be too much for me and I'd die there. Me dying and being buried in Africa? That wouldn't have been so bad. Africa was so good to me for so long.

Photographs

Curtis and Amanda Cressman wedding photo, 1919

Cressman family farm

Elsie and Howard, circa 1928-29

Elsie Cressman graduation from St. Mary's Nursing School, circa 1945

Cressman family, clockwise from centre Joe (foster child), Ruth, Elsie, Howard, Lillian, circa 1926

Green's School, S.S. #4 Wilmot, circa 1933
Elsie, middle row, 3rd from right

Ontario Bible School, Fort Erie, Yearbook "Torch" Committee
Elsie seated 2nd on left

Cressman family, clockwise from left back
Ruth, Elsie, Lillian, and Howard, front
Curtis and Amanda, circa 1938

La Junta Mennonite Hospital, La Junta, Colorado

At the Kansas City Children's Home

Eastern Mennonite College, Harrisonburg, Elsie on the far right

Elsie at Goshen

Women's ward at Shirati Hospital, Tanganyika (now Tanzania)

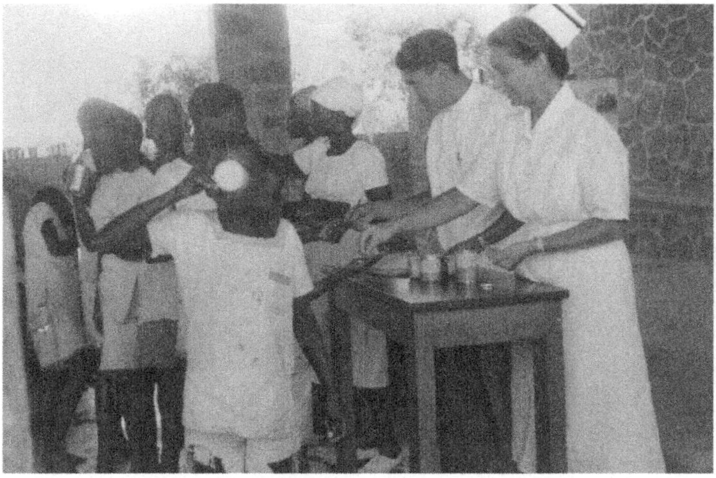

Elsie dispensing medication at the Leprosarium

Leprosy patients arriving at the Leprosarium

Building homes at the Patients' Village

Building homes at the Patients' Village

Elsie's house after the lake rises

Assembled patients waiting for medication at the Leprosarium

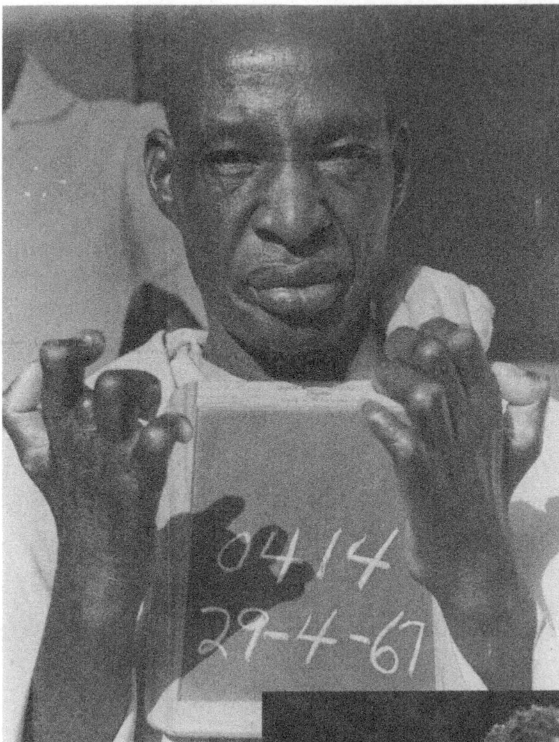

Patient with
Tuberculoid Leporacy

When the patient saw this photo he said, "That was when I was dead."

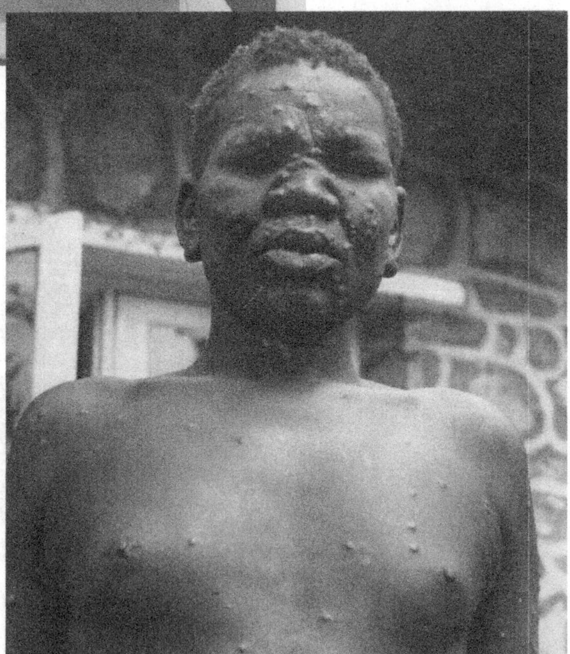

Patient with
Lepromatous Leporacy

Elsie's baby Jerosa

Children being treated for Leprosy

Midwifery School, London, England, 1970-71

Elsie on a bicycle visiting patients throughout London

Two special neighbors

Rusinga Island, Nurses Residence, 1971-75

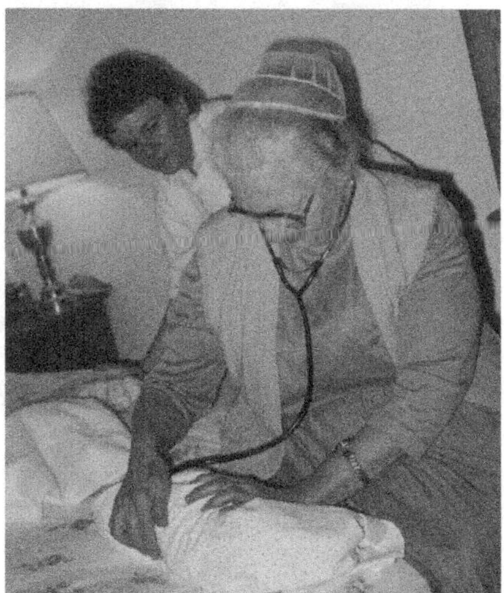

Elsie at work

First birthing home, St. Jacobs, Ontario

The first and last babies Elsie delivered in Canada

Elsie and MPP Elizabeth Witmer at Elsie's retirement, 1998

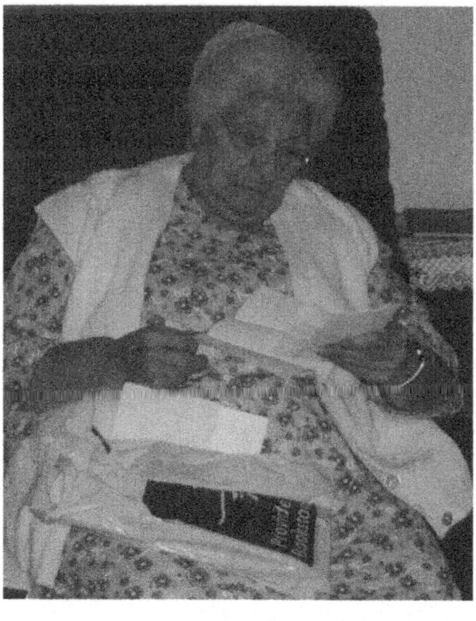

Elsie at home, Nithview Retirement Home

Bibliography

Books:

Barrington, Eleanor. *Midwifery is Catching.* Toronto: NC Press, 1985.

Benoit, Cecilia, Ivy Lynn Borgeault, Robbie David Floyd. *Reconceiving Midwifery.* McGill-Queen's University Press, 2004.

De Vries. *Birth by Design: Pregnancy, Maternity Care and Midwifery in North America and Europe.* New York: Routledge Publishers, 2001.

Dorsch, Victor and Viola. *Life Pilgrimage.* Kitchener: Pandora Print Shop, 2006

Eshelman, J. Lester and Lois Eshleman. *Green Grows the Willow: Shirati Hospital 1935 to 2005 and 1935 to 2007 The Medical Development at Shirati with its International Relationships.* Morgantown, PA: Mastoff Printers, 2007.

Smoker, Dorothy and Merle Eshelman, MD, *God Led us To Somalia.* Salunga PA: Eastern Mennonite Board of Missions and Charities, 1956.

Weaver, Alta B. *Journey Through Time.* Ephrata, PA: Grace Press Inc., 2008.

Wagler, Elizabeth. *Sojourn in Africa.* Harrisonburg, VA: Christian Light Publications, 2003.

Journals:

Caldwell, Brian. "Tragic Error is Cloud in Midwife's Stellar Career". *The Kitchener-Waterloo Record.* April 2002.

Editorial. "Death of Birth Centres is Sad but Inevitable." *The Kitchener-Waterloo Record.* October 6, 1995.

Grange, Michael. "Cuts Anger Advocates of Birthing Centres." *The Globe and Mail.* October 2, 1995.

Hill, Valerie. "Return to Africa." *Waterloo Region Record.*

September 6, 2008 Etcetera W3.

----------"Health Minister Applauds Woolwich Facility as Model for Other Ontario Communities." *Elmira Independent,* February 24, 1992.

Hollands, Judy. "Health Minister Applauds Woolwich Facility as Model for other Ontario Communities." *Elmira Independent,* February 24, 1992.

Hyland-Byrne, Lesley. "Feminists in Power: Women Cabinet Ministers in N.D.P. Government of Ontario, 1990-1995". *Policy Studies Journal.* Volume 25, 1997.

Johnston, Cameron. "Ontario's Birthing Centre Concept May Have Impact on Hospitals, MD's." *Canadian Medical Association Journal.* March 15, 1993.

Loewen Reimer Margaret. "Mennonite Midwife in Forefront of Controversial Cause." *Mennonite Reporter.* Vol. 15, No. 18 September 16, 1985.

Martensson, Erik. "Groundbreaking Ceremony for new Building for WCHC." *Woolwich Observer,* August 11, 2001.

Pink, Dave. "Health-care facility hopes to deliver a Birthing Centre" *The Kitchener-Waterloo Record,* July 21, 2001.

----------"St. Jacobs Midwives Branch Out" *The Woolwich Observer.* January 26, 2002.

Silcox, Nancy. "Bringing Hope and Healing to Africa." *New Hamburg Independent,* September 2, 2008.

Reports, Briefs, Policy Papers, Newsletters:

Brenner, Richard. "Dropping Birth Units Targets Women, Critic says." *The Kitchener-Waterloo Record,* October 7, 1995.

Goer, Henri. "Obstetrics Myths Versus Research Realities A Guide to the Medical Literature." Westport ,Connecticut: Bergin & Garvey

Henderson, the Honourable Justice J.R. "Reasons for Judgment." *Ontario Court File* Number 49 /99 April 16, 2002.

Hutton, Eileen, "Response to Report of Muriel O'Driscoll." August 15, 2001.

Koch, Alice "Descendants of Menno Cressman." 1990.

O'Driscoll, Muriel. "Report Regarding Care Provided by Elsie Cressman." August 15, 2000.

St. Jacobs Family Birthing Home Update. December, 1992.

Ranney, Brooks MD "The Gentle Art of External Cephalic Version." *Department of Obstetrics and Gynecology, the University of South Dakota School of Medicine, The Yankton Clinic.*

Ritz, Jean. "Inquest into the Death of ... " May 20, 21 and June 18, 1982. Kitchener, Coroner Jack Burger. Chief Coroner's Office of Ontario.

No Author:

"Bill 48, An Act to Establish Midwifery as a Self-Governing Profession." Legislature of Ontario, First Reading, April 26, 1984.

"Christine Carere and Paul Joseph Carere by his litigation guardian Christine Carere; Rachelle Judith Carere, by her litigation guardian Christine Carere; April Lynn Carere and Norah Ruth Carere Plaintiffs by her litigation guardian Christine Carere, and Elsie Cressman, St. Jacobs Family Birthing Home Inc. Defendants." The Ontario Superior Court of Justice. June 30, 1999.

"Core Competencies: A Foundation for Midwifery: Education Recommendations of the Midwifery Integration Planning Project to the Interim Regulatory Council on Midwifery." College of Midwives. January 1994.

"External Cephalic Version." *International Journal of Gynecology & Obstetrics.* 72 (2001).

"Guidelines for Registered Nurses Providing Care to Individuals and Families Seeking Alternatives to Childbirth in a Hospital Setting." College of Nurses of Ontario. November 1983.

"Midwifery." *Toronto Women's Health Network Newsletter.* Vol. XXI, #3.

"The Midwife's Model of Practice in Ontario" College of Ontario Midwives. Revised Oct. 1994.

"Proposal to Establish an Independent Health Facility." St. Jacobs Birthing Home Inc. 1994.

"Statement of Claim between Christine Carere and Paul Joseph Carere and Elsie Cressman, St. Jacobs Family Birthing Home." Ontario Court (General Division) January 1999.

"Submission to the Task Force on Midwifery." St. Jacobs Family Birthing Home, Inc. September 25, 1986.

Internet Sources:

Bender, Harold S. "La Junta Mennonite Hospital (La Junta, Colorado, USA)." *Global Anabaptist Mennonite Encyclopedia Online.* 1958. http://www.gameo.org/encyclopedia/contents/L1840.html

Bender, John M. "Miller, Orie O. (1892-1977)." *Global Anabaptist Mennonite Encyclopedia Online.* 1987. http://www.gameo.org/encyclopedia/contents

Boddy-Evans, Alistair. "Timeline of the Mau Mau Rebellion." www.africanhistory.about.com/od/Kenya/a/MauMautimeline.html;

Slaughter, Barbara, "How Britain Crushed the Mau Mau Rebellion." www.wsws.org/articles/1999/spept1999/mau-s15.shtml

Springer, Nelson P. "Mennonite Historical Library (Goshen, Indiana, USA)." *Global Anabaptist Mennonite Encyclopedia Online.* 1957. http://www.gameo.org/encyclopedia/contents/M466842.html.

Yoder, Glen. "Mennonite Children's Home (Kansas City, Kansas, USA)." *Global Anabaptist Mennonite Encyclopedia Online.* 1957. http://www.gameo.org/encyclopedia/M465965.html

No Author:

"About Midwifery: Brief History of Midwifery in Ontario". The College of Ontario Midwives www.cmo.on.ca/midwife_history.php.

"Anesthesia and Queen Victoria." UCLA Department of Epidemiology, School of Public Health. www.ucla.edu/EPI/snow/vicoria.html.

"A Brief History of Shirati Hospital." The Hummels in Africa; Another Nifty Site. www.hummelsinafrica.org/article.php?story+20050511131334356

"A History of Eastern Mennonite University." http://www.emu.edu/history.html

And http://www.gameo.org/encyclopedia/contents/E23879.html

"A History of Goshen College." http://www.goshen.edu; http://www.gameo.org/encycpopedia/contents/G67775.html;

"Kanisa la Mennonite Tanzania.." www.gameo.org./encyclopedia/contents/k365.html

"Leprosy: Hansen's Disease," www.bilkent.edu.tr

"Leprosy." www.nlm.nih.gov/medlineplus/encyc/article/001347htm.

"The Midwifery Model of Practice in Ontario." The College of Midwives of Ontario, Revised 1994. www.cmo.on.ca/downloads/H-MOP.pdf.

"Mount Kilimanjaro National Park." www.tanzaniaparks.com.

"The Official Kenyan Travel Guide and Travel Information Portal." www.magicankenya.com.

"Providing Medical, Educational and Development Assistance to East Africa." www.friendsofshirati.org

The World Fact Book Kenya. www.cia.gov/library/publications/the-world/ke.html.

Made in the USA
Monee, IL
14 September 2026

62974518R00144